ONE-EYED KINGS

ONE-EYED KINGS

BILL WILSON

Copyright © 2008 by Bill Wilson
One-Eyed Kings

ISBN# 978-061523-124-2
Printed in the United States of America

Published by Metro Ministries
PO Box 409
Brooklyn, NY 11237
Web site: www.metroministries.org

TABLE OF CONTENTS

1

THE PROCESS THAT PRECEDES THE POWER

The turning point in the process of growing up is when you discover the core of strength within you that survives all hurt.[1]

FIVE HUNDRED YEARS AGO, the Dutch philosopher, Desiderius Erasmus, coined the much-quoted adage: "In the land of the blind, the one-eyed man is king." I don't think anyone would pick a one-eyed king to take the role of a leader. Only a prophet would choose a handicapped

1

person from among the strongest and the brightest. This leads us to the obvious question. Who are one-eyed kings?

One-eyed kings are ordinary people who have executed extraordinary things. They are not trained. They are not qualified. They have their own sets of problems and issues. However, in spite of their shortcomings and struggles, they become the proverbial one-eyed kings in the land of the blind. They are able to see just a little bit more than the other folks around them.

The value of the one-eyed king is a biblical truth that cannot be denied. Paul put it this way in his ancient letter to the church at Corinth.

> *For ye see your calling, brethren, how that not many wise men after the flesh, not many mighty, not many noble, are called: But God hath chosen the foolish things of the world to confound the wise; and God hath chosen the weak things of the world to confound the things which are mighty; And base things of the world, and things which are despised, hath God chosen, yea, and things which are not, to bring to nought things that are: That no flesh should glory in his presence.*
> —1 Corinthians 1:26-29

God has chosen the weak and the foolish and the humble to become one-eyed kings in a blind world. The Scriptures are filled with illustrations of simple people who accomplished extraordinary things. In the Old Testament, over and over again, God chose one-eyed kings to serve His purposes. In the New Testament Jesus chose one-eyed kings to be His disciples. And today God is still choosing one-eyed kings to fulfill His intentions.

In 1 Samuel 17 we are introduced to the famous biblical story of a then-unknown shepherd boy named David, the youngest of

Jesse's eight sons, and the Philistine army's champion, the giant Goliath of Gath. One of the problems of those who have "grown up" in the church is that they have a tendency to lose perspective of the classic stories of the Bible. They cannot read them in a way that will produce new insights. It is my hope that in this book you will put aside your preconceived notions and open your heart to see the old stories in a new light.

 One does not become a king overnight. It is a process.

Granted, the story of David and Goliath is a great Sunday school story, but it is also a great illustration for all of those who are facing impossible situations. This story is a defining moment in the life of David. It is a moment that could have disqualified him for leadership. From this point forward David's life would change forever. It would be a process that would eventually lead him to a throne.

One does not become a king overnight. It is a process. Shortcuts only lead to blind alleys and dead ends. Knowledge is power but knowledge that is gained too easily is dangerous power. Knowledge from a textbook is different than knowledge gained in a life experience. Process must precede power and position. Process is the training ground that prepares you to experience the power to become a king.

Life is a process. Building a good marriage is a process. Creating a ministry is a process. Developing a successful business is a process. Every successful person has gone through some kind of process that prepared them for their future.

In the life of David we see the value of process—process that paved the way to the power of the throne. The journey from shepherding sheep to shepherding Israel was a long and arduous process fraught with obstacles, betrayal and personal trials. When David started out he wasn't necessarily qualified to be a king, but the choices he made along the way would strengthen his faith and empower him to rule over the nation of Israel.

Faith Empowers You in the Process

When I arrived in New York City more than 28 years ago I did not have a point of reference in order to accomplish the work that God had set before me. Davenport, Iowa is a long way from Brooklyn, New York. That distance is not just calculated in miles. There is a huge cultural difference between those two places. I did not have a clear understanding of what I was walking into when I made the momentous decision to move east. Moving from the land of cornfields to the land of skyscrapers was an act of faith. In those early days I didn't necessarily look at myself as a man of great faith. Nevertheless, it did take faith to move to New York without any money in my pocket and without the support of any church or denomination.

I have to admit that the last thing we need is another message on faith. Everywhere we turn people are writing and talking about faith. Unfortunately much of this contemporary message on faith is focused on prosperity. Preachers describe faith as a pathway to prosperity, fortune, and fame. Certainly God wants to bless us financially. But I also believe that there is a lot more to faith than simply a key to financial blessing.

One-eyed kings have always found a way to conquer their fears and move past their failures.

Without faith it would be hard to get up in the morning. Without faith we would shrink in the face of life's tragedies. Without faith we would give up when faced with disillusionment, betrayal, failure and conflict.

Sometimes life will back you into a corner and when you are in an impossible situation, seeing no way of escape, the temptation is to give up and retreat. Without faith you slip into a ditch of despair and a mire of mediocrity.

One-eyed kings have always found a way to conquer their fears and move past their failures. Faith lifts them above the cloud of uncertainty into a place of quiet confidence—a confidence that is based upon who God is and not their own abilities.

How Do You Find Faith?

All of us are born with a measure of faith but the faith of heroes is a faith that is developed in the midst of life's challenges. Faith that helps you get up in the morning is a *measure* of faith. Faith that enables you to take down giants is *extreme* faith. In order to move into a higher level of faith we must be willing to pass through perilously dangerous valleys and sometimes fight gargantuan giants.

When I came to New York I had a *measure* of faith. In order to stay here for more than 28 years took *extreme* faith. Let me be clear. I did not start out with radical, mountain-moving faith. I grew into that level of faith. Looking into the faces of abused children, drug addicts, prostitutes and gang members required a new kind of faith for me. A *measure* of faith brought me to the city. *Extreme* faith kept me in the city. I needed a new level of faith to believe that God could change these broken and twisted people that I faced every day. It took radical faith to trust God for the finances needed to keep this ministry moving forward.

I have watched my faith develop over the years. Each decision and choice that I made strengthened me in the faith. My confidence grew as I saw God's miraculous deliverance and experienced His many blessings.

Unfortunately many people think their faith can grow without going through this process. They are like the guys in the body-building magazines who are bulging with muscles. Most of them have bulked up through the artificial use of steroids and other supplements. I am a skinny guy, and I remember once trying to bulk up with some of those supplements. Believe me, it doesn't work. You can't look like those guys in six weeks or ever in most cases. Shortcuts do not work and supplements are not a substitute for conditioning and natural strength. You have to have the desire and capacity within you to accomplish the stunning results you see in magazines and competition events.

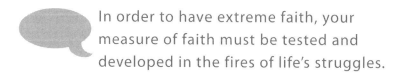

In order to have extreme faith, your measure of faith must be tested and developed in the fires of life's struggles.

What is in you? That is a key question to ask. You may not be able to see who you really are. You are blinded by your own insecurity and the negative comments of others. All of us have capability and potential. That is the starting point, but it's only the starting point. To move from capability to ability will require *development* of your character.

In order to have extreme faith, your measure of faith must be tested and developed in the fires of life's struggles. If we would spend as much time focusing on developing faith as people do in developing muscles in the gym, we would have a lot more heroes of faith. Most Christians have failed to realize that faith is more than just a gift. You don't get it by the transfer from another who lays hands on you. Faith must be developed and strengthened by what athletes call resistance exercise. This is also true for all those who would be strong in faith. It takes exercise in resisting the easy way. The exercise of your faith will develop your faith. Exercise requires facing life's obstacles. You cannot escape the process. The process precedes the power.

You have to work at this. It is not something that is going to drop out of the sky. I wish it did, but it doesn't. When you face economic trouble, family crisis, personal struggles, you have the opportunity to develop your faith.

I have to deal everyday with 40,000 people, maintain 80 buses, vans, and people from many foreign countries who are used to driving on the wrong side of the road. Every day brings a new set of problems and pressures. But I have learned that power is developed in the cauldron of crisis.

In the process of trying to serve God I have developed enough understanding and faith over the years that I believe God is for me. He has proven over and over how much He loves me and how far He is willing to go to protect me. Sometimes when bad things happen in your life you come to believe the lie that God has a vendetta against you. I am here to tell you that He does not have a grudge against you. God is for you!

The problems that intersect your life will test you and develop you for greater things. This is what I call aggressive faith. It is faith that sees the invisible and accomplishes the impossible.

Faith has been talked about so much that we have lost the simple significance of this spiritual truth. Faith is more than an intellectual acceptance of a biblical truth. It is more than positive confession. Faith is an enigmatic thing. It is a mystery. Faith is rooted in your understanding of God and your trust in Him. Faith is the willingness to do what others will not do. Faith inspires you to look at things differently than those around you. Faith empowers you to speak to people with confidence. Faith enables you to defeat your enemies, conquer your fears, and survive your failures.

There is a power that is available to you through faith. The act of faith is a precursor to the power of faith. Faith is a risk but it is a calculated risk based upon the reality of God and His desire to reward those who trust in Him. This kind of faith is expressed in a dynamic display of personal risk in the midst of what seems to be a hopeless situation. If you want to have the power of faith you must be willing to exchange the crowded place for the lonely place. The crowded place is the place of security and safety. The lonely place is reserved for those who are willing to abandon their protected place and embrace the perilous place.

The School of Faith

All of us have been enrolled in the school of faith. When you make the decision that you are going to follow God, you have decided that you are willing to be trained by Him in the way of faith. This faith school is not located in Tulsa, nor is it in Dallas or Colorado. The things you are taught in this school are not learned in Bible schools or seminaries. God is a curriculum designer, and He decides when and what you will learn from these valuable lessons of life.

The school of faith is the school of life.

In 1 Samuel 17 David began his first major course in the school of faith. The first course is entitled: *How Do You Handle Giants?* David had been anointed by Samuel to be the next king of Israel. But it would be 14 years before that anointing became an appointment. There was a process between the anointing and the appointing.

David had to go to school to be prepared to become a king. It was not a school that took place in a royal palace. It took place on the field of battle. There is a process that you must go through. The school of faith is the school of life. Your lessons are presented in the everyday circumstances of your life. You pass or fail depending on how you handle those trials and pressures. David's training did not take place in a classroom. It took place in the heat of a battle, in the solitude of a cave, and in the hopelessness of impossible situations. It doesn't take place in front of the television or a computer. It cannot be learned in a book. You know the story.

David entered this school at a very early age, beginning as a shepherd boy who protected his sheep from wild animals such as lions and bears. He was probably a teenager when he went from fighting bears to slaying giants. He learned how to win what seemed like unachievable battles.

How do you get enough faith to walk into hell with a squirt gun and believe that you are going to win? Where does that kind of faith come from? This kind of faith is rooted in a word from God.

> *So then faith cometh by hearing, and hearing by the word of God.*
> —ROMANS 10:17

When you have a word from God, you will have the faith of God to walk into any situation of life. This kind of faith is empowered in the lives of those who choose to walk through dark and dangerous places.

People of great faith have always had their faith tested. Tested faith produces power. Tested faith brings boldness. Tested faith creates character. David went through the process that produced a seasoned faith. He had received a word from Samuel and that word sustained him in the times of trouble. When I came to New York all I had was the word but the word was enough, because that word sustained me in many dark times.

Facing Your Giants

David learned some valuable lessons about giants when he was a young man. He had already fought some battles before the day he faced off with Gath's favorite son, the giant Goliath. His victories out in the countryside protecting his father's sheep had prepared him to fight Goliath on the battlefield.

The Philistines were the constant nemesis of the Israelites. Once again the Philistines were out for war. The two armies were facing off with one another by the valley of Elah. One of the traditions in those days was that each side would choose a warrior to challenge the other side. Goliath was the choice of the Philistines. Not your typical warrior, the man stood over nine feet tall—taller than any basketball player in the NBA. This giant of a man was wearing military armor that weighed 125 pounds. The point of his spear weighed 15 pounds. This was one formidable warrior! Goliath stood before the Israelite army taunting them in an attempt to lure them into a fight.

David was minding his own business when he heard about Goliath's blasphemous words. This would become a crucial moment in the life of David. He could have simply ignored the situation or he could choose to embrace his destiny and face the giant. You don't go looking for these moments. *They will find you.* David was on his way to bring cheese and bread to his brothers and some cheese for the commanding officers. This teenage boy didn't wake up that morning and decide to go and fight a giant, but divine circumstances had worked together to create a set of circumstances for David. While delivering the food he heard this giant cursing God and yelling obscenities.

 Some people only want to talk about what they would do. Then there are others who put their words into action.

You never know what a day will bring. When I woke up on September 11, 2001, I never dreamed that the events of the day would unfold as they did. That day would produce many courageous acts to be sure. No one had asked for that day, but that day revealed the courage that resides in so many people. It is one thing to talk about faith and it is quite another to demonstrate that faith when life's troubles step into your pathway.

For 40 days the armies of Israel had squared off against the enemy and all that the Israelites had done about it was talk. It was just like some churches are today. They spend hours in meetings talking about something that could have been done months and perhaps even years ago if only someone could make a decision! Some people only want to talk about what they would do. Church leaders are famous for this. Then there are others who put their words into action.

When David heard of the intimidating words of Goliath he boldly declared,

> *And David spake to the men that stood by him, saying, What shall be done to the man that killeth this Philistine, and taketh away the reproach from Israel? for who is this uncircumcised Philistine, that he should defy the armies of the living God?*
>
> —1 SAMUEL 17:26

David's oldest brother was infuriated and probably put to shame by David's words. In anger Eliab snapped back,

> *And Eliab his eldest brother heard when he spake unto the men; and Eliab's anger was kindled against David, and he said, Why camest thou down hither? and with whom hast thou left those few sheep in the wilderness? I know thy pride, and the naughtiness of thine heart; for thou art come down that thou mightest see the battle.*
>
> —1 SAMUEL 17:28

David didn't cower in the corner. Confidently, he responded,

> *And David said, What have I now done? Is there not a cause?*
>
> —1 SAMUEL 17:29

Is there not a cause? It was dawning on David that this was a cause to fight for. He could not slip back into the place of anonymity. He must forge ahead.

Someone heard David's bold declaration and went to King Saul and told him about David. Saul was intrigued by the courageous words of David and summoned him to his presence. When David arrived, Saul was puzzled by David's youth and told him there was no way that he could defeat such a warrior as Goliath. David was not intimidated by Saul's words and the following dialogue ensued:

And David said to Saul, Let no man's heart fail because of him; thy servant will go and fight with this Philistine. And Saul said to David, Thou art not able to go against this Philistine to fight with him: for thou art but a youth, and he a man of war from his youth. And David said unto Saul, Thy servant kept his father's sheep, and there came a lion, and a bear, and took a lamb out of the flock.

—1 Samuel 17:32-34

Where did David find the strength to walk into that valley without the normal weapons of war and believe in his heart that he would come out alive? A lot of us think that we are prepared to face any challenge that might come our way. But it is only when we are threatened by a *giant* of a problem that we will discover just how prepared we are. It isn't in a classroom that you make that discovery. It is on the streets that the revelation really comes.

Keys to Going through the Process

"Faith is a process of leaping into the abyss not on the basis of any certainty about where we shall land, but rather on the belief that we shall land."[2]

Everybody wants to walk on water, but nobody wants to get out of the boat. The process between the jump and the land is based upon the willingness to take the risk. All that the Israelite army wanted to do was *talk*. David was appalled by their position. He stood up to them and asked them what they were doing. What was everyone doing? David was thinking, *Why are these guys allowing Goliath to get away with his taunting? Why is no one standing up? What is up with this?* I wish I had ten people who had the audacity of David.

This kind of person is an individual who has walked through the process. For David there were three distinct parts of the process. The process that he went through would lead him from a *measure* of faith to *extreme* faith.

The process that leads to power is the route that will lead us to a place of quiet resolve and courageous acts. When I first came to New York City I encountered a host of preachers who told me that I could not accomplish my vision here. In the more than 300-year history of New York City no one had ever attempted to do what I proposed to do. No one thought that my plan to reach the children of this city could ever work. The struggle I faced seemed to be an impossible battle. Like the army of Israel they told me that the struggle was too big and the enemy was too strong.

How did David acquire this kind of faith? If it is a process, what brings it to pass? I don't put myself in the category of the faith that David exhibited, but both of us faced the same process that brought us to victory time and again. Here are three keys I have discovered that have helped me to move through the process to the power.

1. Nurtured in Solitude

> *"I love people. I love my family, my children...but inside myself is a place where I live all alone and that's where you renew your springs that never dry up."*[3]

Have you ever been in a situation that was life threatening? Have you ever looked at an enemy and wondered if you would survive that day? Have you ever faced an obstacle in your life and wondered how you were going to get out?

Elijah did. One of the great conflicts in Hebrew history is the battle between Jezebel, the notoriously evil wife of Israel's wicked king, Ahab, and Elijah, who was considered the greatest prophet of the Old Testament. Jezebel was a Phoenician princess, the daughter of King Ithobaal I of Sidon when she married Ahab. Many historians agree that she was the most imperious, unscrupulous, vindictive, determined, and devilish woman of her day.

Under Ahab and Jezebel's reign, temples of Baal operated in Israel, with the blessing of royal patronage. Further, the queen used her control over Ahab to lead the Hebrew children into sin and subject them to unspeakable tyranny. She slaughtered the prophets of Israel and in 1 Kings 18, Elijah challenged 450 of her prophets, who were devoted to Baal, to a test, ending in their death and exposing their god as powerless.

Jezebel was incensed at the death of her prophets and focused her rage toward Elijah. She sent a messenger to tell him that she knew where he was and before the day's end she was going to kill him. Few of us have ever faced that kind of wrath! I find it curious that she sent a messenger. If she knew where he was, why didn't she just send an army to overtake and kill him? I think she was just pushing his buttons.

I have experienced that several times. People want to use their threatening words to induce fear in you in order to get you to back off. Well, it worked. Elijah ran for the hills. The same guy who called fire down from heaven a couple of days before now ran for his life in terror because some woman threatened him.

What's the lesson? You had better be careful what you listen to! When I was in my twenties I had to visit a speech therapist. This was the result of working summers back in my home church and preaching outdoors without a microphone four or five hours a day for five days a week. At the time I had no idea that I was supposed to be breathing from my diaphragm. I was speaking right at the top of my voice, and I paid the price for it. The first thing the therapist wanted to do was to give me a hearing test. I found that interesting. Hello!! I have a speaking problem, not a hearing problem. The therapist went on to say that it had been discovered that people who struggle with speaking might have a hearing problem.

Bad hearing can cripple our speech. When we let negative and fearful words enter our conscious thoughts, we subject ourselves to the possibility that our actions will be negatively affected. The dripping of negative speech into your ears can wear away at your faith. Words have a powerful influence on our lives. That is why I am deeply concerned about the kind of music that kids are listening to these days. It is no wonder that music with violent lyrics leads to violent actions.

Elijah finally found himself huddling—crouched down and trembling, I'm sure—in a cave. But he was nurtured in that cave by a still, small voice. That voice gave him the courage to abandon the place of panic and embrace the process that leads to power.

David was also a man who was nurtured in solitude. He had found that place long before his confrontation with Goliath. Alone on the hillsides of his family's land he had discovered the *power of privacy.* As a shepherd he spent many days alone with his sheep. He had no one to talk to. All alone he experienced the power of the quiet place.

We, in the western world, know very little about this place of solitude. We surround ourselves with music, television, computers and mindless mutterings. I was recently on a six-hour flight from Los Angeles back to New York. From the moment we entered the plane the woman in front of me began talking. She continued with her incessant talking throughout the entire flight. She was a talking machine. What can you talk about to total strangers for six hours? I don't know.

This is a simple illustration of our fear of silence. We are afraid to be alone with our thoughts. David did not have that problem. He loved the sounds of silence. They spoke to him of the love and greatness of God. The quiet place inspired him for the many psalms that he would write. It was in the lonely places that he practiced with his faithful slingshot. It was in the quiet place that he heard God's voice and grew in strength. He was nurtured in solitude.

Without knowing it David was preparing himself for that historic day when he would take down the biggest giant in his life. Albert Einstein said that the monotony and solitude of a quiet life stimulates the creative mind. The God we serve is a God of creativity. But in order to enter into that divine creativity we must silence the sounds around us. It is in that quiet place where we will hear the still, small voice. That voice will empower you and me to face our own giants.

An article in USA Today stated that people who overthink things do not get dementia as easily as those who don't. So if you don't want to go nuts, shut up and think!

2. Strengthened in Conflict

Remember how Saul questioned David's ability to fight this giant? Saul was basically saying, "What gives you the idea that you are qualified to go out and fight Goliath?" How did David respond? He talked about his encounters with a lion and a bear. These were very ferocious opponents. He had fought a lion and a bear, and he was not afraid to go out and face this enormous enemy of Israel. Many of us have been fed a treacherous lie. We have been led to believe that when we come to Jesus everything will be okay. We will have no more problems. Then when we get ourselves into a battle we are taught to "rebuke" our enemies.

 The process of pain is the way of those who will walk with Jesus.

The sad thing is that we were never taught that there would be battles. The process of pain is the way of those who will walk with Jesus. These conflicts are a key part of the process that brings us from weakness to strength. If we choose to avoid the conflict, then to that degree we will remain weak. What will you do when you get a doctor's report that says you have cancer? What will you do when you get a phone call and hear that someone you love has died? Will you run or will you fight?

If you avoid the lion and the bear you will not be prepared for the giant and you will die in the valley of Elah. You will die a spiritual death. I don't enjoy traveling through the valley of darkness. I don't like rejection and betrayal. I don't like facing financial struggles. But I have learned that the course of conflict will lead me to the place of strength. Extreme faith is developed and fashioned in our struggles.

You do not get strength for a battle; you get strength from the battle. It is in the midst of the battle that we discover strength. I know that my battles have strengthened me for the work that God has given me to do. That is why I can talk with a calm resolve when all hell is breaking loose around me. For 40 years of ministry, I have been tackling trouble and overcoming obstacles. I have learned to trust God for the purchase of a $4.5-million-dollar building. I have learned to remain at peace when trials are swirling around me. I have fought a "lion" and beaten him, and I have fought a "bear" and survived.

Extreme faith does not just fall out of the sky. It is the result of a process. It is nurtured in solitude and strengthened in conflict. Like David, I have learned to reject Saul's armor and put on God's armor. I have learned to use creative methods to reach out to people—methods that others would not use. You have to learn what will *fit* you. What others do just might not fit for your circumstances. Don't let others try to define you or shove you into the box of their experiences. You have to learn to fight your own battles in your own way.

3. Proven in Hopelessness

Hopeless situations become opportunities for faith to be manifested and your character strengthened. When you arrive at the place where the battle looks like it is hopeless, that is what separates the liars from the buyers, the pretenders from the contenders. David was a contender. Incensed by the taunts of Goliath, David was ready to face what seemed like a hopeless situation.

> *Thy servant slew both the lion and the bear: and this uncircumcised Philistine shall be as one of them, seeing he hath defied the armies of the living God.*
> —1 SAMUEL 17:36

David left the courts of Saul and marched toward the valley with his slingshot and his staff. There was a reason for the staff. I'll try to get to that at another time. Upon hearing the insulting jeers of Goliath, he picked up five smooth stones out of a brook. Five smooth stones would be all that was necessary to deal with this situation. Why did he need five stones? Goliath had an armor bearer, and he had some sons. David wanted to be prepared just in case he needed a couple more shots for the enemy's friends.

There he was—just a boy—facing this enormous giant of a man. Goliath couldn't believe his eyes. Was this a joke? What a scene— one small kid with a slingshot and five stones facing a nine-foot tall giant. This was an unbelievable situation. But David had been prepared for this hopeless set of circumstances. The hopeless situation became a hopeful situation because his faith was in the God of hope.

> And the Philistine said unto David, Am I a dog, that thou comest to me with staves? And the Philistine cursed David by his gods. And the Philistine said to David, Come to me, and I will give thy flesh unto the fowls of the air, and to the beasts of the field. Then said David to the Philistine, Thou comest to me with a sword, and with a spear, and with a shield: but I come to thee in the name of the LORD of hosts, the God of the armies of Israel, whom thou hast defied.
>
> —1 SAMUEL 17:43-45

Standing in an unrealistic place, David was positive and prepared. He would bring down this giant.

> This day will the LORD deliver thee into mine hand; and I will smite thee, and take thine head from thee; and I will give the carcases of the host of the Philistines this day unto the fowls of the air, and to the wild beasts of the earth; that all the earth may know that there is a God in Israel.… And David put his hand in his bag, and took thence a stone, and slang it, and smote the Philistine in his forehead, that the stone sunk into his forehead; and he fell upon his face to the earth. So David prevailed over the Philistine with a sling and with a stone, and smote the

Philistine, and slew him; but there was no sword in the hand of
David. Therefore David ran, and stood upon the Philistine, and
took his sword, and drew it out of the sheath thereof, and slew
him, and cut off his head therewith. And when the Philistines
saw their champion was dead, they fled.

—1 Samuel 17:46, 49-51

David wanted his generation to know that
God is real and that if they put their trust in
Him He would bring them into their destiny.

David turned what appeared to be a hopeless situation—an
unwinnable battle—into a total victory. His desire was not to prove
how great he was. His passion was that all the earth would know
there is a God in Israel. What do you want? Really, not the right
answer, but what's really in your gut. Are you searching for fortune
and fame? Are you looking for a nice house, a wonderful family,
and a big bank account? Not David. He was not seeking his own
glory. He wanted his actions to bring glory to God. He didn't want
to impress the king or his army. He wasn't looking for a reputation,
nor seeking notoriety. David wanted his generation to know that
God is real and that if they put their trust in Him He would bring
them into their destiny.

Let me just remind you that giants come in all shapes and sizes.
Your giant may not be a nine-foot tall Philistine. But you will face
your own giants. Sometimes they come in an urgent phone call.
At other times they come in the form of an x-ray. Often a giant
appears with the sound of screeching tires on a crowded highway.
Monsters try to lure you away into places of fear and dread. Giants

are trying to impose their hateful will upon your life. If you've lived long enough, you know this.

One-eyed kings are people who know about struggle and heartache. They have walked through sad and sorrowful times. But they are people who have made the choice not to run. They have faced their giants with a sling, a stone and a staff. They have been nurtured in solitude, strengthened in conflict, and proven in hopelessness. They have discovered that the process that precedes the power is a tremendously blessed highway on which to travel.

2

THE PROCESS THAT PRECEDES THE PARTNERSHIP

I will have no man work for me who has not the capacity to become a partner.[4]

Now these be the last words of David. David the son of Jesse said, and the man who was raised up on high, the anointed of the God of Jacob, and the sweet psalmist of Israel, said, The Spirit of the LORD spake by me, and his word was in my tongue.

—2 SAMUEL 23:1-2

WHEN A PERSON IS on their deathbed they usually count their words carefully. The mind floats over your past life reminiscing about the days gone by. Before the darkness of death makes its final intrusion one has a clearer understanding of what is really important: Family, close friends, the memorable events of your life. Usually in those times you grow in your appreciation for the people who meant the most to you.

I've had the honor of hearing many people's last words just before they died. I have not forgotten them. Whether it is a woman dying on a dirt floor in Haiti, or a great preacher—a person's last words are important. Their words are indelibly etched upon my heart. I remember when a missionary called me to her house after she found out that my mother was found dead. I came to the house and she was sitting in an old rocker and began to talk. "I need to tell you something." Her eyes were closed. She had a deteriorating disease above her eyelids and could no longer keep her eyes open. I believe the disease was called myasthenia gravis. It is a neuromuscular disorder that causes a fluctuating weakness and fatigue of certain voluntary muscles, including those in the eyelids. I literally took her eyelids and held them open so that she could see me while she spoke dynamic words of encouragement to me. She told me that whether I ended up being a minister, a missionary, or someone who just wanted to do something for Jesus Christ, to never ever leave the presence of God. Sadly, she died shortly after that experience, but I will never forget those words.

Last words are important words. The greater the person, the more meaningful his words become. In the dying days of Moses, he called the children of Israel to his side and left a prophetic blessing for each of the twelve tribes. The last words of Jesus on the cross are permanently inscribed upon each one of our hearts. In a letter to Timothy, at the end of his life, Paul said that he had fought the good fight, he had finished the course, and he had kept the faith. Witness the power of the words of these famous people, uttered at their death:

> *"The paper burns, but the words fly free."* (Rabbi Akiba ben Joseph at the stake, when the Torah was also burned.)

> *"Now comes the mystery."* (Henry Ward Beecher)

> *"It is well, I die hard, but I am not afraid to go."* (George Washington)

> "Have you made your peace with your God?" *"I never quarreled with my God."* "But aren't you concerned about the next world?" *"One world at a time."* (Henry David Thoreau)[5]

The Forming of a Partnership

Nearing the end of his life David reflected back over it all. In this moment of contemplation he thought of his friends—his mighty men of valor. These were the men who formed a partnership with David on the battlefield that led him to the throne. They were there in his darkest hours and stood faithfully at his side. Amongst the armies of Israel these were the ones who captured David's attention and formed his elite guard.

> *Moreover the Philistines had yet war again with Israel; and David went down, and his servants with him, and fought against the Philistines: and David waxed faint. And Ishbibenob, which was of the sons of the giant, the weight of whose spear weighed*

three hundred shekels of brass in weight, he being girded with a new sword, thought to have slain David. But Abishai the son of Zeruiah succoured him, and smote the Philistine, and killed him. Then the men of David sware unto him, saying, Thou shalt go no more out with us to battle, that thou quench not the light of Israel.

—2 SAMUEL 21:15-17

When David stood before the giant Goliath, he stood alone; it was a *personal* battle. That glorious victory set the stage for his journey to the throne. Here in this passage we can identify the fact that a transition has taken place. No longer will David have to fight alone. He has gathered those to his side who have become partners with him, and they will now fight his battles with him. We have moved from the personal to the corporate. T. Austin Sparks said it best in his message on David's mighty men:

"You know that David himself first came into view in relation to the throne in connection with this original (and what we might call, inclusive) giant. It was in his victorious combat with Goliath that David was first taken account of publicly, and this marked his first step toward the throne of Israel, in relation to which he had been anointed. Now we have moved on some considerable distance, and the security of that throne is seen to be the issue at the time of these mighty deeds... In David's case, it was personal. He fought a lone battle with Goliath; he was a lone figure on that field. When the giant challenged, all the people fled, but David moved out alone to accept that challenge and to answer it. But here, in the portion of the record with which we are now dealing, everything is corporate; but it is the same issue. It is all gathered up into a company. The one giant, the inclusive giant, has been fully dealt with and beheaded, but he has left

some of his offspring, and they are all giants; and now the giant in corporate expression is being met by the corporate expression of the throne."[6]

This kind of transition does not happen overnight. It is a process. David's mighty men will prove themselves to David on the battle-field. These are not men who received their training in an Israeli war college. It was not academic training in a classroom; it was practical training in the combat zone. They learned their trade at the side of David fighting the enemies of Israel. They would eventually enjoy the glory of being at his side when he was inaugurated as king because they were willing to stand at his side when he was betrayed by Saul and hounded by the enemies of Israel. They had *earned* the right to be his partners because they were *willing* to embrace the process.

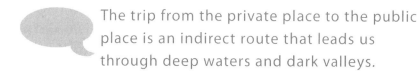

The trip from the private place to the public place is an indirect route that leads us through deep waters and dark valleys.

If you are willing to go through the process, you'll get to the place God designed for you. But you don't just show up one day and get a reward. You don't just wake up one day and say, "I am here. I am ready for ministry." In the days of the Roman Empire, a soldier had to serve for 20 years before he became a centurion. The trip from the private place to the public place is an indirect route that leads us through deep waters and dark valleys. If you have the option of the elevator or the stairs, always take the stairs. You'll understand what it takes to get where you want to go.

It is a long, arduous process and for some it takes years. It was 40 years for Moses. Moses made one bad choice and because of that bad choice, he paid the consequences for 40 years, but it did not fully disqualify him. David was not a perfect man, neither were his mighty men. They all made their mistakes, but they learned from their mistakes. I've had my failures, and so have you. We must never forget that our failures do not disqualify us, they determine us. We are trained by how we respond to our failures. Failure is never final with God. Ultimate victory is dependent on how we handle those failures.

From the Private Place to the Public Place

Your starting point is as important as your ending point. David began his life in the hidden place, hiding in caves and valleys. He was willing to go through the process that would eventually lead him to the throne. Authority is not something that should be given to novices. Plato, in his book *The Republic,* talks about the rigorous training of the Guardians in the private place. He envisioned that they would be trained till the age of 50 before they were allowed to assume any kind of leadership in Greece.

David dealt with his issues in the private place so that he would be prepared to be a ruler in Israel. Unfortunately, too many of God's people seek shortcuts to fortune and fame. They think that a little education will prepare them for the public place. Why are we surprised when these people fail?

God will hide you in the house until you are ready to come out. If you feel as though you have been hidden, you don't feel like you are being noticed, you feel that you have so much to contribute but nobody cares, that's okay. You need to realize that there is a process that you must go through before your calling can be manifested. Better to deal with your weakness in the private place than to have it exposed in the public place. I always tell my staff, "the higher you climb, the more your underwear shows!"

What is Greatness?

I was in Malaysia a couple of years ago, and while I was signing books and talking a young man came up to me and he said very seriously, "I want to be a mighty man of God, but I don't think I have what it takes. I don't think I have what it takes to be that kind of man." That is interesting. He didn't believe he had what it takes to be what God had called him to be. We can interpret his insecurity in one of two ways. Either he did not have enough faith in God that he could rise to the level of greatness that God had for his life or, in the face of the great men of God he had known, he didn't think he could attain that level of greatness. Few of us can ever imagine ourselves as great men and women of God.

What defines greatness? How would you define a great and mighty man or woman of God? How would you characterize greatness if someone asked you for a clarification? Is greatness defined by a successful career, recognition by your peers, or material things like money, houses and a certain level of notoriety? Is greatness to be defined in the context of material things and public recognition?

Jesus was once asked by his disciples, *At the same time came the disciples unto Jesus, saying, Who is* **the greatest** *in the kingdom of heaven?* (Matthew 18:1, emphasis added). Jesus' response contradicts all human definitions of greatness. He responded to the question in this way, *And Jesus called a little child unto him, and set him in the midst of them, and said, Verily I say unto you, Except ye be converted, and become as little children, ye shall not enter into the kingdom of heaven. Whosoever therefore shall humble himself* *as this little child, the same is greatest in the kingdom of heaven* (Matthew 18:2-4).

In the mind of Jesus greatness is defined as servanthood.

On another occasion this topic came up again as the disciples were arguing over who would be the greatest among them. With clarity and certainty Jesus responded, *And he said unto them, The kings of the Gentiles exercise lordship over them; and they that exercise authority upon them are called benefactors. But ye shall not be so: but he that is greatest among you, let him be as the younger; and he that is chief, as he that doth serve* (Luke 22:25-26).

In the mind of Jesus greatness is defined as servanthood. This concept runs upstream against the river of current thought in the secular and religious worlds. In the community of men, both secular and religious, we define greatness in the terms of fortune and fame, power and recognition. We define greatness in the terms of winning the game of competition, rather than succeeding at the game of companionship and partnership.

Metro Ministries is a worldwide training center. People come from every corner of this planet to receive ministry training. What they learn here is the significance of serving others, not for personal gain, but for the glory of God. Likewise, David's mighty men had gathered around David in order to serve him and the divine destiny on his life.

We need to understand what they possessed once they got into that position of partnership with David. What did they possess? There must be a process that proves the content of character that is in their lives. Greatness is developed in the process. Charles de

Gaulle, 18th President of the French Republic, once said that greatness is a road that leads to the unknown. David's mighty men followed him into the unknown and in that place they manifested their strength.

David's Mighty Men

The older I get the more careful I am about the people I allow into my life. I am careful who I spend time with, for good reason. I understand the power of influence. Henry Drummond, the great English spiritual philosopher, said that all men are mirrors. By this he meant that we are all the reflection of the influences that we allow in our lives. Here is how he described those influences. *"The books he has read, the people he has met, the influences that have played upon him and made him the man he is—these are all registered there by a pen which lets nothing pass, and whose writing can never be blotted out."*[7]

David selected his men wisely. He knew that the people who surrounded him would determine his ability to fulfill God's call on his life. In 2 Samuel 23, at the end of his life, David introduced us to those mighty warriors. In both this chapter and in 1 Chronicles 11 they are described as "The Thirty." They are David's choice men. As they died they were replaced by others who had shown valor in their service to David. That might be the reason for the irregularity of the lists in these two chapters.

This is a very interesting group of folks. They were the kind of people that I should have hired a long time ago. I needed them when I started this ministry. In order to qualify to be among "The Thirty," you had to distinguish yourself in the tough times. These were not ordinary folk. They were men of stature…men of strength...men of war...men who were not afraid to stand up in the face of the enemy.

Look at this group! David's mighty men were not seeking rewards. They served David because of their great love and respect for him. David had encircled himself with a group of men who were loyal to him. They didn't have the assurance that he would be the king but they trusted him and would serve him to the death. They were not just faithful to him when he had the kingdom; they were true to him *before* he was king.

A lot of people want to be around you when you are the king. The reasons are obvious. As king you have much to offer them—position, prestige, and power. But would these people associate themselves with you if you were not the king? Would they comfort you in a cave? Would they stand with you on the battlefield? Would they stand fast when the enemy is approaching? Would they be there when you don't have a paycheck to offer them? This is the true test of greatness and loyalty. Unfortunately, at times, some of those who say they are with you really aren't. David's mighty men were with him in the tough times. They proved themselves with their steadfastness and their swords. They were not concerned about their own personal interests. Their hearts were focused on David, and they were committed to making him king.

The Power of Three

These be the names of the mighty men whom David had: The Tachmonite that sat in the seat, chief among the captains; the same was Adino the Eznite: he lift up his spear against eight hundred, whom he slew at one time. And after him was Eleazar the son of Dodo the Ahohite, one of the three mighty men with

David, when they defied the Philistines that were there gathered together to battle, and the men of Israel were gone away: He arose, and smote the Philistines until his hand was weary, and his hand clave unto the sword: and the LORD wrought a great victory that day; and the people returned after him only to spoil. And after him was Shammah the son of Agee the Hararite. And the Philistines were gathered together into a troop, where was a piece of ground full of lentiles: and the people fled from the Philistines. But he stood in the midst of the ground, and defended it, and slew the Philistines: and the Lord wrought a great victory.

And Abishai, the brother of Joab, the son of Zeruiah, was chief among three. And he lifted up his spear against three hundred, and slew them, and had the name among three. Was he not most honorable of three? therefore he was their captain: howbeit he attained not unto the first three. And Benaiah the son of Jehoiada, the son of a valiant man, of Kabzeel, who had done many acts, he slew two lionlike men of Moab: he went down also and slew a lion in the midst of a pit in time of snow: And he slew an Egyptian, a goodly man: and the Egyptian had a spear in his hand; but he went down to him with a staff, and plucked the spear out of the Egyptian's hand, and slew him with his own spear.

—2 SAMUEL 23:8-12; 18-21

Before David introduces us to "The Thirty," he talks fondly about two sets of three who distinguished themselves from "The Thirty." The first triumvirate of men was selected because of their power. The second trio of men was selected because of their passion. The power of three has great biblical significance. The tabernacle was built in three parts: outer court, Holy Place, and most Holy

Place. Jesus rose from the dead on the third day. Paul said that there are three qualities of life that stand out among all others: faith, hope, and love. There is a certain mystery and strength in the three...always has been.

The first set of three is distinguished by their power. They embodied the spirit of the true warrior: strength, courage, and loyalty. The first of the three was Adino. Adino had employed his spear against eight hundred men, killing them all in one historic battle. He didn't let up until there were no opponents left. I don't know if that connects with you, but when you are outnumbered 800 to one, that would be classified as a really tough fight. Very tough! I've been in quite a few street fights, but I don't know if I would be up for that or not. I don't like the odds on that battle!

I feel like I've been up against 800 warriors sometimes, but not in this context. I have faced what seemed like insurmountable odds—situations where I didn't think I would be able to achieve a victory. In those times I did find the empowering presence of God that enabled me to forge ahead and succeed when everyone—and I mean everyone—thought I would fail.

Then in verse nine we read about Eleazar who fought so hard that his sword nearly became a part of the palm of his hand. The grip on his sword was so tight that it could not be separated from his hand. Have you ever held on to something for so long that the intenseness of it is painful? Many times I have driven to Florida, where I'm from, and after a while my hands would feel like they had become a part of the steering wheel. I needed to keep moving. Eleazar had fought so long that his sword had become an extension of his body. This is what I call commitment to a cause. Too many of us would give up in the face of such intense struggle, but not Eleazar.

The final of the three is Shammah. Another conflict had ensued and the battle was over a little plot of ground. The object they were contesting was "a plot of ground full of lentils," a very little part of the inheritance that God had given Israel, but one containing food for the people. The enemy was seeking to deprive them of the field and its crop. Shammah stood in the middle of the field and preserved it for God's people. Shammah gained recognition because of his fidelity to David and his love for God's people.

Passion for the King

David's final thoughts now turned to an event that was forever carved into his memory. The story highlights another set of three. These three are not noted because of their skill with the sword but with the compassion of their spirit.

We have seen a guy who killed 800 warriors in one single battle. We watched as another fought for so long that his hand was united to his sword. The final guy rose up in a time of crisis and destroyed the Philistine force that was seeking to interrupt one of their food lines. All of these guys performed these unusual feats of war and now we are introduced to another group of men who are not warriors, but men of great compassion, loyalty and love.

What does it take to be a mighty man of God? That is an interesting question and cannot be answered in one set of exclusive characteristics. On one hand, a mighty man of God is one who is distinguished by brute force and dynamic strength and, on the other hand, we can describe mighty men as those who are singled out by their compassionate loyalty and caring acts. Now to the story! What set these guys apart from the other thirty?

And three of the thirty chief went down, and came to David in the harvest time unto the cave of Adullam: and the troop of the Philistines pitched in the valley of Rephaim. And David was then in an hold, and the garrison of the Philistines was then in Bethlehem. And David longed, and said, Oh that one would give me drink of the water of the well of Bethlehem, which is by the gate! And the three mighty men brake through the host of the Philistines, and drew water out of the well of Bethlehem, that was by the gate, and took it, and brought it to David: nevertheless he would not drink thereof, but poured it out unto the Lord. And he said, Be it far from me, O Lord, that I should do this: is not this the blood of the men that went in jeopardy of their lives? therefore he would not drink it. These things did these three mighty men.

—2 Samuel 23:13-17

Why did these three men get on this list? They are differentiated from among "The Thirty," not for capability, but because of their compassion. David was sitting with these mighty men in a cave, hiding from the Philistines. The Philistines were pressing the battle all around them and had even taken over David's blessed city of Bethlehem. In a moment of contemplation about the battle, he allowed his thoughts to become public. His men heard him longingly express his desire for a drink of water from the wells of Bethlehem. He wasn't talking to his men. He was talking to himself. He wasn't asking for his men to go out and risk their lives just so he could have a drink of water. David would never do that.

He was not in a place of position; he was in a place of peril. The situation seemed hopeless, but he was still surrounded by those who were committed to him, not because of the promise of reward, but because of the *passion of devotion.*

This is a leader's dream—men and women who will not desert them in the time of trouble.

When you get into trouble, it is always interesting to see who is left standing with you. When others are leaving, the money is running out, and popularity has disappeared, it is nice to know that there are still those who will not abandon you. This is a leader's dream—men and women who will not desert them in the time of trouble.

David and his men were about a half mile north of Bethlehem close to the area where he grew up. He knew this area. He was thinking back on his childhood. When you get older that is what you will do. Why? After you have had so much responsibility, so much pressure to perform, after you have had to be the bread winner, the soul winner, the game winner, it is nice to be able to just get somewhere and think back to the times in your life when life was simple.

I understand how David felt. There was a time when I did not have 170-plus fulltime staff that could not get along with each other because they were young and lacked maturity. There was a time when I was alone and did not have the financial responsibility that I have now. I wasn't responsible for a television show. I wasn't traveling around the world starting these Sunday schools. It was a much simpler time.

Do you have a place like that? A place in your mind where you can go and be a kid again? In the midst of challenging situations we are often, nostalgically, carried back to the days of our youth when life was easier and less complicated. It is a sweet place.

And David was sitting there in a cave longing for a great drink of water from a great well that he remembered drinking from as a child. He was thinking, *I wish I could do that again.*

Three of his friends in the cave overheard his spoken thoughts and got a stupid idea. *Let's leave the security of the cave and go get David a drink from those wells.* David didn't ask them to get it. He didn't command them to get it. Can't you imagine these guys' conversation? *Let's go get the water! What will it take? Let's see, all we have to do is battle our way through this Philistine army, drop a bucket into the well and get a cup of water, and then battle our way back to the cave.* It was an insane idea! But selflessness overtook logic.

Can you imagine this scene? They got the water. One of the guys was carefully holding the cup of water while the other two led the way back through the Philistine army. I would like to know which guy was carrying the cup of water because that's where the pressure was.

The Glory of Honoring Another

Now it is an interesting thing to me in that we really don't know what motivated them, but for whatever reason these three guys just decided to do it. Maybe this is where I am intrigued with this whole thing. What force creates that kind of passionate loyalty? What motion generates that kind of devotion to another person? What kind of love will cause someone to step out of his own concern for his own life in order to serve the desires of another? It's obvious that selfishness is rampant in the church. Too many are more concerned about serving their own desires than serving the purposes of another. We are more concerned about developing our own ministry, rather than enhancing the work of another. The only answer can be selfless love—love for another that overrides your passion for your own desires.

Some people are amazed by my love for Tommy Barnett, pastor of one of the largest churches in America. To this day when I am with him I still carry his briefcase. I am several years younger than he is. I have had more than a few people ask me why I do that. They tell me that I am on the same level as him. My ministry is every bit as big as his. They don't understand the power of honor. I honor and love Tommy Barnett. He has always been there for me, encouraging and caring about me. I will always prefer him above me. I owe him.

I often think about my home pastor. Sadly, he committed suicide, but you know what? I will always respect and love him. I owe him—I always will. He saw something in me that no one else saw. He gave me an opportunity that no one else would have ever given me. Even in his death, I owe him.

The only thing that elicits reverence and respect, honor and deference is compassion. It is this kind of compassion that will change a world that is controlled by ruthless self-love.

Commitment to the Wishes of Another

And David longed, and said, Oh that one would give me drink
of the water of the well of Bethlehem, which is by the gate!
—2 SAMUEL 23:15

These mighty men were not only concerned with David's *words*, but also with his *wishes.* If David had commanded them to go and get him a drink of water they would have done it. But their loyalty went beyond commands. Their loyalty did not need a command.

God is looking for those who do not need to be commanded to serve Him.

One of the problems with Christianity is that we applaud talent over devotion and ability over affection. We put talent on the platform and relegate devotion to the pew. This is not the way of God. God exalts passion over potential. God chooses ordinary people to perform extraordinary things. God chooses people who are willing to go through the process in order to partner with Him in His purposes.

God is looking for those who do not need to be commanded to serve Him. Their service is based upon devotion, not duty. I recently went through a situation that illustrates the absurdity of letting your life be controlled by Law, as opposed to love. We had just bought a new building that had a freezer. We desperately needed to use this freezer for ice cream that was being delivered to us. Even though we had not yet taken occupancy of the building, we thought that the owners, who were Jewish, would allow us to use the freezer. Nope, we were not allowed. Why? Because our ice cream was not kosher! What? I did not even know that there was kosher ice cream. How do you get kosher ice cream? You need one of the priests from the Orthodox University to come and bless it. We are not talking about some pig. We are not talking about lamb chops. They would not allow us to use their freezer for our ice cream. They chose Law over love.

Christians aren't much better. At times the legalism of our religion keeps us from doing what is right and good. The Law builds such a huge wall sometimes that we lock ourselves into our own dopiness. I don't know if that's a word, but it is now. This construct of piety keeps us from seeing the good that we can do for others. We are so locked into our own little religious world.

These three men took the initiative. They were not concerned about their own wishes—they were tuned into the wishes of their king. They were willing to leave the enclosed walls of security and face the outside world because of their love for the king.

The Value of Love

And the three mighty men brake through the host of the Philistines, and drew water out of the well of Bethlehem, that was by the gate, and took it, and brought it to David: nevertheless he would not drink thereof, but poured it out unto the LORD. And he said, Be it far from me, O LORD, that I should do this: is not this the blood of the men that went in jeopardy of their lives? therefore he would not drink it. These things did these three mighty men.

—2 SAMUEL 23:16-17

Imagine how these three devoted soldiers must have thought about David's joy when they delivered the water to him! No! Imagine their bewilderment when David took the cup and poured the water upon the ground! They have just risked their lives because of their great love for David and for their desire to fulfill his wishes and now he poured out the water on the ground. How are we to interpret David's actions? Is he an insensitive, ungrateful king? Or, is there something that we are missing in his actions?

The answer to this question is found in his own words: *Be it far from me, O LORD, that I should do this: is not this the blood of the men that went in jeopardy of their lives?* And the verse concludes, *Therefore, he would not drink it.*

David was not just moved by the deed, but he was moved by their devotion. Their love for him washed over David in overwhelming waves of respect and gratitude. These were men who were willing to risk their own lives in order to fulfill the simplest wish of their friend. David was stirred by their affection and felt unworthy to drink from the cup that came with such a price.

He was overcome by their willingness to be a servant. You have to understand, not all sacrifices are the same. Just because you *think* you are making a sacrifice does not mean that you are really making a sacrifice. The offer of money when you are rich is not necessarily a sacrifice. Jesus understood the truth that not all gifts are the same.

> *And there came a certain poor widow, and she threw in two mites, which make a farthing. And he called unto him his disciples, and saith unto them, Verily I say unto you, That this poor widow hath cast more in, than all they which have cast into the treasury: For all they did cast in of their abundance; but she of her want did cast in all that she had, even all her living.*
>
> —MARK 12:42-44

These men had given what the church has come to call their "widow's mite." They had proven their love for David with an unrequested, selfless act. He knew they were willing to sacrifice their lives to do something that he had not even asked them to do. Overwhelmed by their sacrifice and feeling undeserved of their love, he could not partake of the cup.

Your service for God must be founded in your devotion to Him.

They had gone through a process that proved their partnership with David was not forced; it was willingly offered. In order for you to enter into that kind of co-labor with Christ you will also have to go through the process. Saying "yes" to Jesus *must* be demonstrated in more than your words. Your passion for Him will be proven in the process.

Your service for God must be founded in your devotion to Him—a devotion that is revealed in the process of life. Your motivation must transcend the desire for fame and fortune. In the face of insurmountable situations in your own life that zaps all of your energy, always remember that the process leads to a partnership. Everything we face, whether it be financial, job, family, marriage, sickness, fear, loneliness, or betrayal will lead us to the place close to the side of God, partnering with Him in His desires and not your own.

3

THE PROCESS THAT PRECEDES THE PREPARATION

"What we do upon some great occasion will probably depend on what we already are; and what we are will be the result of previous years of self-discipline."[8]

L IFE EXPERIENCE LEADS TO leadership preparation and entrance into a life that is already prepared for you. Assimilation of information is not enough. Knowledge can only be transformed into power when that knowledge is absorbed and incorporated into your personal life. That is why I continue to assert that Bible colleges and seminary training is not enough to fulfill your future. There is a process you must go through in order to reach your divine destination, the life that is prepared for you by God.

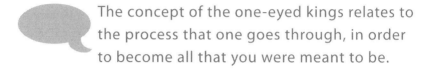

The concept of the one-eyed kings relates to the process that one goes through, in order to become all that you were meant to be.

Knowledge must be functionally focused into the process of life. The proof that we have gained knowledge is manifested in our actions. If we continue to make the same mistakes then we only prove that we did not get the message. I have no interest in delivering a word that does not change people's actions.

The concept of the one-eyed kings relates to the process that one goes through, regardless of your insecurities and inabilities, in order to become all that you were meant to be. This is a process that precedes power and promotion. It is a process that leads you into all that has been prepared for you—a process that precedes the preparation. You might not realize it yet but *there is something very wonderful that has been prepared for you.* Unfortunately, many never enter into that world of their prepared future. They allow the roadblocks of pride, failures, and insecurities to prevent them from securing God's plan for their lives.

Joshua was a one-eyed king—someone who never bought into the typical system. He was very happy to be the second man. He was happy to serve God by serving Moses. He was very good at being number two. His preparation under Moses would eventually prepare him for a promotion that was critical in the history of the Jewish people. Joshua learned a valuable lesson while serving

Moses—*how we serve **under** a leader will determine how we serve **as** a leader.*

Joshua was not a wimp, nor was he the ground for others to tread upon. But he did understand the importance of learning servanthood. He comprehended this divine principle established in the teachings of Jesus. Learning to serve will prepare you for learning to lead. Joshua was not looking for a promotion or a pay raise. Joshua was not secretly seeking to undermine Moses in order to take his place. Maimonides, a Jewish sage in the twelfth century, once said that one of the great sins is to gain respect through another's disgrace. There were those, like Korah, who sought to destabilize Moses' authority, in order to establish their own. But it was not so with Joshua.

Here is another key to leadership. Your disloyalty will never open the door that your loyalty will inevitably open. Joshua's loyalty to Moses would open a door for him to enter into what had already been prepared for him.

A Future Prepared for You

Moses my servant is dead; now therefore arise, go over this Jordan, thou, and all this people, unto the land which I do give to them, even to the children of Israel.
—JOSHUA 1:2

I find it interesting that sometimes you are prepared and sometimes you are not, but even when you think you aren't, maybe you really are. One-eyed kings in the land of the blind have a prepared future for them, something they could never realize with their natural vision. Joshua was not looking to be a leader in Israel. He did not have a hidden agenda while serving Moses. He did not think that his position at the side of Moses would lead him to a position over Moses. Joshua simply served Moses. His loyalty was highlighted by his self-sacrificing service. Maybe no one else saw his loving commitment to Moses, but the most important thing was that God saw it. God saw it and out of all the people He could have picked, He chose Joshua.

No preparation here, just *Moses is dead!* When a great leader has passed away, in that vacuum is a potential for crisis. Moses had led Israel out of slavery. He had introduced them to the power of God at the Red Sea and in the wilderness. Moses had delivered to them the Laws of God. But now Moses was dead. What would Israel do? Who would lead them into the next phase of their history? Who would fill this vacuum? It must be someone who has gone through the process of preparation. It cannot be a novice.

Joshua was divinely selected because he was gracefully prepared for this promotion. In serving Moses he had learned to serve God. Now was his time to enter into the future that had been prepared for him.

I know a lot about the responsibility of picking the right person for the right job. I don't believe in natural selection. I believe in divine selection! I don't necessarily look for the most gifted. My eyes are upon those who have proven themselves by correct choices and inspired actions. I can teach a trustworthy person the skills they need for a certain task. I cannot teach someone to be trustworthy or loyal. You have to kiss a lot of frogs to find the prince.

This was not a job for an ordinary person who was getting ready to take some people on a magical mystery tour. We are talking about leading an entire generation of people into the future. In their hands is the future of God's purposes. The hope of Christianity was riding on this man who was going to be placed in a position of leadership and a one-eyed king is always the best selection for a job like this. I am sure that Joshua did not feel prepared or worthy. But, in spite of his fears and insecurity, he was the right man at the right time for a noteworthy task.

The Promised Land was already prepared for Joshua's leadership. The land had been prepared and readied, but a leader was needed—one who understood proper authority, one who was not an apprentice, and one who was not afraid of the challenge.

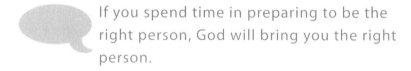

> If you spend time in preparing to be the right person, God will bring you the right person.

The land was always out there. It had been prepared for them, and now it would appear that God's people were finally ready. After forty years of taking laps around the mountain they were now primed to enter into the place that had been prepared for them.

The Process that Leads to the Preparation

I hope you know by now that just because something has been prepared for you does not mean you are going to wake up one day and walk into it. Marriage is a good example. Just because you are old enough to get married does not mean you are prepared for marriage. In Proverbs 18:22, Solomon said that the one who finds a wife finds a good thing. He was not saying that she was already a wife. That is adultery. What he was saying was that the one who finds a woman who is constantly preparing to be a wife has found a good thing. Too many young people are seeking to get married before preparation to be married. We spend more time and money on preparation for the day of the wedding than we do on spending time and focus on the life after the wedding. No wonder so many marriages end in divorce. If you spend time in preparing to be the right person, God will bring you the right person. It's not rocket science.

Joshua didn't waste his time trying to be the leader. He allowed himself to be trained for that leadership.

> *And it came to pass, when the priests that bare the ark of the covenant of the LORD were come up out of the midst of Jordan, and the soles of the priests' feet were lifted up unto the dry land, that the waters of Jordan returned unto their place, and flowed over all his banks, as they did before.*
>
> *And the people came up out of Jordan on the tenth day of the first month, and encamped in Gilgal, in the east border of Jericho. And those twelve stones, which they took out of Jordan, did Joshua pitch in Gilgal. And he spake unto the children of Israel, saying, When your children shall ask their fathers in time to come, saying, What mean these stones? Then ye shall let your children know, saying, Israel came over this Jordan on dry land.*
>
> *For the LORD your God dried up the waters of Jordan from before you, until ye were passed over, as the LORD your God did to the Red sea, which he dried up from before us, until we were gone over: That all the people of the earth might know the hand of the LORD, that it is mighty: that ye might fear the LORD your God for ever.*
>
> —JOSHUA 4:18-24

Remember the Red Sea? Israel had already seen a miracle at the parting of the Red Sea. The experience at the Jordan would be different. At the Red Sea the waters parted before they crossed over. At the Jordan priests had to step into it. As they stepped toward the water they crossed over on dry ground. The miracles of the past are not enough for our future. Just because God did something one way does not mean He is going to do the same thing again. Your journey to leadership will also be unique. This time, *the leadership had to get their feet wet.* They had to step in. Then the people were lifted up onto dry land. Nineteen miles up river God had blocked the waters. I don't know how long it takes for water to recede 20 miles downstream, but it doesn't happen immediately. Those guys were standing in the water for a while with their pants rolled up…everybody looking at them like they were a bunch of knuckleheads.

"What are you doing?"

"I am standing here."

"For what reason?"

"Because God said to."

"Okay. Well, you look like an idiot."

However long it took for the water to dry up from upstream 20 miles away, these guys were standing there. It took a certain faith to leave Egypt and cross the Red Sea. It would take a different measure of faith to cross the Jordan into their land of promise.

Because of sin the Jewish people had been wandering for 40 years in desert places. God was now ready to deliver them from the reproach of the desert experience. After they crossed over the Jordan they traveled for about five miles and made camp. The place where they encamped was called Gilgal. Gilgal is about two and a half to three miles northeast of Jericho, the place of the first major battle in the land of promise. Now they had the opportunity to step into the Promised Land—the place of their destiny, the place of fulfilling God's plan for their lives. Their history of failure was behind them. Their future was before them.

They had just come out of 40 traumatic years of dealing with a lot of junk, of paying for their disobedience, paying for their lack of faith, dealing with their own stupidity, and now they had arrived at the land that God had promised to them. All of us have been at that point. We have come out of great trials and crises. We know that something is prepared for us. We can feel it. But the question still lurks in the shadow of our thoughts. Are *we* prepared for *it?*

Do you understand what I am saying? Are you prepared for that which has already been prepared for you? God has prepared something for you but here is the haunting question. After 40 years of wandering, are you prepared?

What was the significance of Gilgal? Gilgal was the place of final preparation for the future events that would soon unfold before them. Again, life is a process, character development is a process, relationship is a process, marriage is a process, ministry is a process, raising children is a process. You don't immediately step into your future.

When I perform weddings I often tell the bride and groom that you don't cleave to your future mate in a one-hour ceremony. You can leave quickly, but you can't cleave quickly. The Bible says a man should leave his mother and father. You can leave that relationship quickly. Cleaving, however, takes years. It takes years of making this new life work. It takes years of seeking to understand one another, bond to one another and build a life together.

The Scripture says that they came up out of Jordan on the tenth day of the first month and they encamped in Gilgal, in the east border of Jericho. *Encamped*—this is actually a word used for rest, but it is more than that.

For 40 years they had been seeking, searching, wandering, struggling, and limping along as they searched for their future as the people of God. Now they were at Gilgal. It is unclear how long they stayed there. It could have been as long as ten years. For the first time in Canaan they celebrated the Passover.

The day after Passover, they began to enjoy the fruits of the land that had been promised to them hundreds of years before. They ate unleavened bread and grain from the new land. It was at Gilgal that the manna ceased. They would now work for their own food. It was at Gilgal that circumcision was renewed. This was the place of new beginnings and a new commitment to God was forged. They stayed in Gilgal to heal and to make preparations for the next stage of their journey.

Gilgal was a place of new preparation. At Gilgal they would rest and reflect. At Gilgal their shame would be rolled over. At Gilgal they would pause to remember the goodness of their God.

A Place of Resting and Reflecting

Israel had been wandering around the wilderness for 40 years. This unfortunate detour filled their minds with uncertainty and vacillation. Just as their past had imprisoned them, their future eluded them. Now on the verge of entering a new place they would need to take time to rest. They needed a place of rest, but another word that fits there is *reflect*. They needed some time to rest and reflect after their time of fighting and wandering, struggling and feeling sorry for themselves—after realizing that they had missed it.

 In the midst of personal battles there has to be a time where you can pull back and look at your life.

They must reflect on themselves, on the past mistakes, on how far their lives had come. They would spend a moment of deliberation on where they were going next. There was much that they needed to process.

In the midst of personal battles there has to be a time where you can pull back and look at your life. There has to be a time to take stock of what has gone before. John Locke, the British philosopher, once noted that the custom of frequent reflection would keep a person's mind from running adrift and call their thoughts home from useless and inattentive roving.

I have noticed that when I give myself time to reflect, I see things I have not seen before. Sunday nights are my typical time for reflection. I will find an appropriate place to get alone and think about the events of the weekend and the previous week. It's Sunday night, and it's probably the only time in my entire week when I don't feel the pressure of one more service and facing one more decision. For those few short hours I have a window of time to pull back, look at my life, and ponder how things went, what I could have done better, what should have been done differently, and just to relax in my spirit.

You have to remember that Gilgal was not their destination. Don't miss this! Gilgal was not their destination. There is a danger in seeking the secret place. The danger is that we will not leave that place. As precious and important as that place is, it is not our final place. It can quickly become a place that prevents us from facing the future that awaits us.

It is easy to make some alternative choice become your destination. All of us need a secret place, like Gilgal, where we can reflect on our lives, but Gilgal was never designed to be your destination. Monasteries are not our destiny. A sabbatical rest can be a good thing, but I have found that many people never return from that place. There are still battles to be fought and ground to cover. The resting place is a place of reflection but it is only a refuge on the way to our final victory.

This was the day that God chose to roll away Israel's reproach and remove their shame.

Reflection will prepare you to step into the next dimension of your journey but do not be tricked by the enticement of the reflecting stream. Use it to encourage yourself and prepare yourself to enter into God's new place for you, and then move on.

The Place of Rolling to Remove

And the LORD said unto Joshua, This day have I rolled away the reproach of Egypt from off you. Wherefore the name of the place is called Gilgal unto this day.

—JOSHUA 5:9

Gilgal means "rolling." This was the day that God chose to roll away Israel's reproach and remove their shame. He would roll away the reproach of Egypt and the shame of their failures in the wilderness. They must be freed from their slave mentality and released from their shame mindsets.

In order to embrace their future they must be freed from the past. God brought them to this place because they were still not ready for the Promised Land that He had prepared for them. They were still living in bondage though they were no longer captives. They could not get past the shame that had been produced by their captivity in Egypt and their calamity in the desert.

All of us have had to deal with the sounds of shame that create such discord in our souls. There is a significant difference between shame and guilt and embarrassment. Shame has to do with who you *are.* Guilt has to do with what you *do* and the resulting embarrassment when you fail. Guilt refers to something that someone has done—taking responsibility for some offense or wrongdoing. "I am guilty. I did it, and I am guilty." Webster's Dictionary defines *embarrassment* as "to cause to feel self-consciously distressed; disconcerted; confounded; confused; mortified." I define *embarrassment* as "I was guilty and you found out, and now I look like an idiot." Unfortunately, we've all been there.

"A pervasive sense of shame is the ongoing premise that one is fundamentally bad, inadequate, defective, unworthy, or not fully valid as a human being."[9] In order to have success in life you must free yourself from the bonds of shame. You must be free from the twisted idioms of a slave mentality that is held captive by self-loathing.

God says, "I am going to roll this thing away from you." The first thing you will learn about shame is this: You don't have the power to free yourself from its ghastly clutches. You cannot escape the Egyptians' finger-pointing, constantly being brow-beaten by a group of people who berate you and hold you down.

If you really are who you say you are, then why are you still doing the things that you do? That is what shame is—it is the inconsistency between who they said they were and what they did. God brought them to Gilgal to remove the shame and reproach of the inconsistency in their lives. The inconsistency between what we profess we are and what we do is a heavy burden that only God can take away.

The problem is that I am what I am, and I did what I did. Do you see the conflict? If I am what I say that I am, I should not have done what I did. I am caught in the vortex of who I am and what I do and the shame that this whirlpool produces.

The good news is that God has a place called Gilgal just for you and me. It is a place where He will roll away our reproach. It is a place where we will see that God's grace is greater than our shame. It is a place where our sins are forgiven and our failures are reversed. Gilgal is a place of hope and expectation, but you have to get to that place yourself.

Camels are what we call beasts of burden. They carry the burdens that do not belong to them. When an owner of a camel takes a stick and taps the camel on the knees, the camel will drop to its knees so that its burdens can be literally rolled off of it. This is what God wants to do in your life. He wants to roll away the shame and reproach that you have picked up after all these years in "Egypt" and in your own personal "wilderness." You can't go into your land of promise with all that weight and burden.

You have come out of Egypt, but Egypt has to come out of you. As you read this book, you may realize that you still have a little bit of Egypt left in you. You lived there for so long that you have developed a slave mentality and a shame mindset. I want you to know that God has prepared a blessed place for you. That place is the place of promise, the place where you will find your future. But before you can enter that place, you must allow Him to roll away your dishonor, disrepute and disgrace.

A Place of Reminding and Remembering

And command ye them, saying, Take you hence out of the midst of Jordan, out of the place where the priests' feet stood firm, twelve stones, and ye shall carry them over with you, and leave them in the lodging place, where ye shall lodge this night.
—Joshua 4:3

From the place of Gilgal, the Jewish people would go forth and fight battles. There were a lot of enemies on their way to their Promised Land. God wanted them to set up a physical memorial that would remind them of the greatness of their God. So He instructed Joshua to take twelve stones from the Jordan River that they had just crossed, and put them in a lodging place. Every time they came back from the rigors of battle, they would see the twelve stones and be reminded to remember their significance.

 As we celebrate the table of the Lord we remember His sacrifice that procured our salvation and opened a way for us to experience the power of God for ourselves.

Epicurus, the Greek philosopher once wrote, "Do not spoil what you have by desiring what you have not; remember that what you now have was once among the things you only hoped for." Memory is the conscious ability to recall personal experiences and inspired words as we confront new challenges. God knew that as they went out to face new battles they would need to remember the day that He was with them and by His power helped them cross over the Jordan River.

This is why Jesus established the Lord's Supper and commanded us to do this in remembrance of Him. As we celebrate the table of the Lord we remember His sacrifice that procured our salvation and opened a way for us to experience the power of God for ourselves.

We are all prone to forget. Humans have very short memories. We get so wrapped up in the things of life that we forget what God has done for us to get us to this point. We hyper focus on the present and we forget the victories of the past. The battle will never end, and sometimes you might have to take some stones and build a memorial in your life to help you remember the goodness of God. People in ministry and leadership can develop amnesia in a heartbeat.

This is why I go back to the corner every Christmas, where my mother abandoned me. Why do I do that? Because it is really easy to forget where you came from. I have a lot to be thankful for, and so do you. That is why an evangelist named Gypsy Smith (1860-1947) kept a wooden clothespin in his pocket. The early days of his ministry had been very difficult. The preachers in the city were afraid of him and would not invite him to preach in their churches. His message was too hard and too radical, but he would not allow them to deter him from his mission. He made a decision. He would go to the streets and preach the Good News. Soon, he had more people in the street than there were people in the churches.

Can you believe this? The people in the churches got mad at him because of his success. Sometimes a guy can never win no matter what he does. Gypsy Smith had thousands of people out on the streets, but he never wanted to forget his starting place. He would say to himself, "I told these people I had a message. I told them I had something to say. Now the folks are coming to hear me." In the midst of feeling pretty good about his success, he would put his hand in his pocket and touch that clothespin. What was the significance of the wooden clothespin? It reminded him that before his success as a preacher, he was once the maker of wooden clothespins. He had worked in a factory making little wooden clothespins. Gypsy Smith's life seemed meaningless. But a day came when God directed him to go into the land of promise. In that land he became successful, but he never wanted to forget where he came from.

The early 13th century conqueror and military leader of much of what we now know as Asia, Genghis Khan (1162-1227), conquered over half of the civilized world. In spite of the fact that he had most of the world's gold, silver, and wealth at his fingertips, he always slept in a *jurt*—a circular felt tent—and ate all of his meals from a wooden bowl and drank from a wooden cup. He valued the simplicity of his Mongolian culture and never allowed the spoils of the western culture to overshadow the roots of his homeland *steppes* (the Mongolian plains).[10]

To this day, Genghis Khan is regarded as one of Mongolia's greatest and most legendary leaders. He is responsible for the emergence of the Mongols as a political and ethnic identity. He reinforced many Mongol traditions learned from his childhood and provided stability and unity during a time of great uncertainty. He is also credited for the introduction of the traditional Mongolian script and the creation of the *Ikh Zasag*, the first written Mongolian law. Although there is a chasm in the perception of his brutality, Mongolians maintain that the historical records written by non-Mongolians are unfairly biased against Genghis Khan; and that his butchery is exaggerated, while his positive role is underrated.

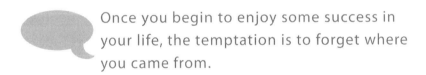

Once you begin to enjoy some success in your life, the temptation is to forget where you came from.

At the time of his death, the Mongol Empire stretched from the Caspian Sea to the Sea of Japan. The People's Republic of China considers Genghis Khan to be an ethnic minority hero. The rationale for this claim is the fact that there are more ethnic Mongols living inside the PRC than outside, including Mongolia itself. While Genghis Khan never conquered all of China, his grandson, Kublai Khan, completed that conquest and established the Yuan Dynasty that is often credited with reuniting China. There has also been much artwork and literature praising Genghis as a great military leader and political genius, although his legacy remains a topic for argument to this very day.[11]

Once you begin to enjoy some success in your life, the temptation is to forget where you came from. You start feeling like you've made it on your own, without God. You forget that you had some serious scars in your life. You forget that you got some wounds along the way. You cannot have plastic surgery for those scars. They run just as deep and cause just as much pain. Only God can remove the reproach and you must never forget that moment.

Every time you win a battle, you need to go back to Gilgal and remember how your life started. You need to be reminded that before God rolled away the burdens in your life, you were nothing.

We must never take the goodness of God for granted. We're not here because we are so smart. We're not here because we are so strong. We're not here because we are so cute. We are here because of the grace and goodness of God.

I understand that God has prepared something wonderful for me. I understand that when you begin to enjoy the blessings of your calling that you forget. When I began this journey at 19, I thought I had the world by the tail. I thought that when I started speaking at some of the biggest churches in the world, I had arrived. I was special. It wasn't long until I realized that I did not have the world by the tail.

Potential does not secure success. Talents do not guarantee victory.

I have learned that your gift will open the door for you, but you have to have enough character to discover a power and strength to stay in that place. You may be very gifted. You may have great natural ability. Here is the sad part. I have seen talented people who are living destitute under a bridge. I have seen gifted people who are begging for bread on street corners. I have seen prostitutes who have squandered their gifts. I have seen too many people waste their abilities in the wrong place. Potential does not secure success. Talents do not guarantee victory. Our potential must be transformed into reality and the Spirit of God must harness our talents. We must learn that the power of God and the wisdom of God is the key to true spiritual success. The place that God has prepared for us can only be reached by the power and direction of God.

When we started the work here in New York City we had 1,010 kids in Sunday school and the very first day, we became the fastest growing Sunday school in the USA. Number one in one day. I thought I was really something, and I knew more than most people. Guess what? That was almost 30 years ago, and I have learned a lot in 30 years. I have to remember that I was nothing when I started out. I have to remember that it was God's power and wisdom that brought me to this place. I must be humbled by the grace of God.

I have fought a lot of battles in my lifetime, but I must still remember where I came from. I must remain in a grateful place. I must keep my eyes on God, rather than on myself. Every time I drift from that memorable place, I get into trouble.

Gilgal reminds us that there is no life back in Egypt. Gilgal reminds us of our failures in the wilderness. But, Gilgal also reminds us that we once crossed a mighty river. Gilgal reminds us that God has taken away our shame. Gilgal reminds us that we have won some battles along the way.

Gilgal reminds us that life is a process. But, Gilgal gives us hope that through the process we will reach the place that God has prepared for us.

4

THE PROCESS THAT PRECEDES THE PUNISHMENT

The deepest human defeat suffered by human beings is constituted by the difference between what one was capable of becoming and what one has in fact become.[12]

HOW COULD SOMEBODY WHO had every chance to succeed—talent, charisma, anointing, opportunity, and position—fail to succeed? How is it that a person who had everything going for him, ended his life in suicide?

We will find the answer to that question in the life of the first king of Israel—King Saul.

> *And the Philistines followed hard after Saul, and after his sons; and the Philistines slew Jonathan, and Abinadab, and Malchishua, the sons of Saul. And the battle went sore against Saul, and the archers hit him, and he was wounded of the archers. Then said Saul to his armourbearer, Draw thy sword, and thrust me through therewith; lest these uncircumcised come and abuse me. But his armourbearer would not; for he was sore afraid. So Saul took a sword, and fell upon it. And when his armourbearer saw that Saul was dead, he fell likewise on the sword, and died. So Saul died, and his three sons, and all his house died together.*
>
> —1 CHRONICLES 10:2-6

A Jewish Tragedy

The ancient philosopher Aristotle (384 BC-322 BC), in describing Greek tragedy, said that tragedy is a form of drama exciting the emotions of *pity and fear*…involving persons renowned and of superior attainments.[13]

Greek tragedy, like Shakespearean tragedy, includes poems and stories of people who experienced heartbreaking endings to their lives. The story of King Saul is a Jewish tragedy. Saul was head and shoulders above all his compatriots and had such a promising life set out before him.

> *Now there was a man of Benjamin, whose name was Kish, the son of Abiel, the son of Zeror, the son of Bechorath, the son of Aphiah, a Benjamite, a mighty man of power. And he had a son, whose name was Saul, a choice young man, and a goodly:*

and there was not among the children of Israel a goodlier person than he: from his shoulders and upward he was higher than any of the people.

—1 Samuel 9:1-2

What better choice for the first king of Israel? On their first encounter the prophet Samuel had a word for this gifted young man. God had told Samuel that a young man would come to him and he would anoint him King of Israel.

Now the Lord had told Samuel in his ear a day before Saul came, saying, To morrow about this time I will send thee a man out of the land of Benjamin, and thou shalt anoint him to be captain over my people Israel, that he may save my people out of the hand of the Philistines: for I have looked upon my people, because their cry is come unto me. And when Samuel saw Saul, the Lord said unto him, Behold the man whom I spake to thee of! this same shall reign over my people.

—1 Samuel 9:15-17

You know how it works. Saul was God's choice for Israel. He was a godly man. He was a good-looking man. He was a strong and anointed man. Saul appeared to be the best choice for a decisive job. In this chapter we will explore how one man, with such great *potential,* could ruin his life. We will see how potential is not enough. We live in a sad world where too many people waste their God-given potential.

Saul was not killed on the field of battle. Saul committed suicide on the field of battle. On that tragic day Saul and all of his sons fell at the feet of the enemies of Israel. The last surviving member of the house of Saul, Mephibosheth, son of Jonathan and thus, grandson of Saul, was not killed that day because he was not in the battle. He was only five years old when his father and grandfather perished at Mount Gilboa. Mephibosheth fell in fleeing with the others of Saul's household and suffered injuries which left him crippled for life.

All the men of Israel saw that Saul was dead and they fled. When the Philistines came to strip the slain, they found Saul and his sons. After they stripped him they took his head and his armor, and sent them to the land of the Philistines. They put his armor in the house of their gods and fastened his head to the temple of Dagon.

> If you know history you will understand prophecy. Those who don't study history are doomed to repeat history.

That's how they handled their enemies in those days. It's kind of like church today. These traditions remain the same in the Middle East to this very day. In the war in Iraq the enemy took our guys, cut their heads off and hung them from bridges. We shouldn't have been surprised. That is their culture, as horrific as it is.

If you know history you will understand prophecy. That is why I don't study prophecy. I study history instead. History gives us the clues to understanding prophecy. Theologians have their prophetic charts and charm us with their mesmerizing words on the end times. The sad thing is that they don't understand history and therefore cannot effectively interpret the times in which we live. Someone once said that those who don't study history are doomed to repeat history. History repeats itself because we're too stupid to learn the first time. The history of Israel is rich in knowledge that would help us in these times.

The books of Samuel, Kings and Chronicles are the Synoptic Gospels of the Old Testament. What this means is that these books are a divine synopsis of the early history of the Israeli people. It is not a glorified view of Israel's history. In these stories we get the good, the bad and the ugly. We see their leaders and people exactly as they were, with all their weaknesses and strengths.

Death of a Dream

All of us have dreamed of the possibilities that might come to us because of our potential and the possibilities that might open before us. Unfortunately, the pathway to the fulfillment of that dream is laden and laced with all kinds of danger. He who is not aware of the danger is doomed to fall prey to its tragic traps. Punishment does not happen automatically. The death of a dream is a subtle process that is activated by dishonorable decisions and defective deeds.

Saul was gifted and anointed. That is why David refused to take advantage of Saul even when he had the chance to kill him. He understood the principle that you should not touch God's anointed. Saul was compounding his mistakes but David refused to join in on Saul's stupidity. Saul's pride and willful actions would lead him to his own death. The man of promise became the man of punishment. He was not punished *for* his sins. He was punished *by* his sins. Augustine wrote in his *Book of Confessions* that every inordinate affection is its own punishment.[14] Every wrong thing you do will come back to bite you. For those of us who have been bitten, we understand that very well.

There is a huge difference between Saul and David. Both men had their flaws and inconsistencies. The difference between these two men is revealed in how they handled those flaws and failures. Saul sought to hide his sin. David chose to confess his sin. We all fail. That is an inevitable truth. The key to longevity is in how we handle our failures. As highlighted in his words in the book of Psalms, David over and over confessed his sins before God. Saul chose to cover up his sin. His cover-ups would eventually lead him to the death of his dream.

All failure or success comes down to the heart. David had a humble heart while Saul had a proud heart. Saul had the appearance of royalty while David had the appearance of a shepherd. This is an important truth as we look at the process that leads to punishment. Outward appearance is deceptive. Just because you appear to be good does not mean you are good. Paul put it best when he wrote, *For we commend not ourselves again unto you, but give you occasion to glory on our behalf, that ye may have somewhat to answer them which **glory in appearance, and not in heart*** (2 Corinthians 5:12, emphasis added).

The Enemy Within

In Israel's history we discover clues to Saul's failure. In that history we learn about the enemy that sought to bring down Saul. When the Israelites crossed the Jordan River they were confronted with a new enemy, the tribes that lived in the land of Canaan. It was about 2047 BC when they approached the Promised Land. On their way to their future, five tribes endeavored to frustrate the Israelites as they sought to establish themselves in Israel. When Saul became king they were his constant nemesis.

The first tribe we read about is the *Ishmaelites.* The Ismaelites trace their roots back to Hagar who had an illicit relationship with Abraham. Ishmael was wild and wayward. After leaving the camp of Abraham he became a true son of the desert. Like Jacob, he had twelve sons who became known as the Ishmaelites. It is interesting to note that it was the Ishmaelites who bought Joseph and took him to Egypt where he became a Jewish slave.

> *Then there passed by Midianites merchantmen; and they drew and lifted up Joseph out of the pit, and sold Joseph to the Ishmeelites for twenty pieces of silver: and they brought Joseph into Egypt.*
>
> —GENESIS 37:28

Many believe that the sons of Ishmael became the Arabs of today, continuing to be a thorn in the side of Israel.

The war between the Jews and Arabs has been going on for centuries.

The second of these troublesome tribes was the *Edomites.* The Edomites were descendants of Esau, the brother of Jacob, who sold his birthright to his brother for a bowl of soup. The Old Testament book of Numbers, chapter 20 relates how the Edomites would not allow the Israelites to pass through their territory on the way from Egyptian bondage to the Promised Land. *Edom* means "red." Red was the color of the soup that Esau sold his birthright for. Let me reiterate. If you don't understand history you will not understand the cruel conflict in the Middle East. This is not a new war by any means whatsoever. The war between the Jews and Arabs has been going on for centuries. There is a built-in animosity that goes back for thousands of years.

The next two tribes were the *Moabites* and the *Ammonites.* They were descendants of Moab and Ben-Ammi, the sons of Lot, and lived on the eastern side of the Jordan River. We know quite a bit about Lot from the Old Testament. He was the nephew of Abraham who separated himself from his uncle and settled in Sodom. Lot was attracted to the beauty of Sodom and envisioned a better life for himself and his family in this ungodly city. The sin of Sodom was so horrific that God decided to destroy the city, in spite of the intercession of Abraham. Lot finally fled the city before its destruction.

Fleeing the city Lot's wife looked back to catch one more glimpse of the city she loved. In that glance she was turned into a pillar of salt. (See Genesis 19:26). The interesting note is that she turned into salt at the Gates of Zoar, a small town which was about 35 to 38 miles away from Sodom, a couple of days' journey from Sodom. She had plenty of time to separate herself from Sodom and yet she still took that tragic look. Lot was left with his two daughters. The Bible tells us that he ended up having sex with both of them. As a result of this incestuous relationship (see Genesis 19:30-38), both daughters became pregnant and each had a son. The older daughter's son was called Moab; he is the father of the Moabites. And the other was called Ben-Ammi, who became the father of the Ammonites.

It is from within that we encounter our most formidable enemies.

The final tribe that caused Israel so much frustration was the *Amalekites*—a nasty bunch of fierce desert warriors who occupied the regions around Sinai. The Amalekites were descendants of Amalek, the son of Eliphaz, who was Esau's first-born son, which means he was Isaac's grandson. The seeds of revenge sprouted in the garden of Esau's grandson. The Amalekites were the first to come into contact with the Israelites (see Exodus 17:8), vainly opposing their march at Rephidim, not far from Sinai. Agag was a mighty king of the Amalekites in the time of Saul and we will meet him again later on.

Here is an interesting note. All of these tribes came from within the seeds of Abraham. *They were birthed from struggles that came from within.* They were distant relatives of the Jewish people. Our greatest enemies are not those outside our gates. Our greatest enemies live within our own gates. It is from within that we encounter our most formidable enemies. Those enemies are often people with unresolved conflicts in their lives. The seeds of destruction are within their belly. They can be gifted people but their gifts have never come under God's control.

Great gifts, great minds, but never submitted to the purposes of Christ. All of the enemies that are constantly trying to keep God's people from fulfilling their dreams are within our gates. They are the Ishmael and Judas groups that secretly plot our destruction. They are traitors to the cause of Christ. These are the ones we must be aware of—those that are of us, but never for us. The only time The Great Wall of China was breached was when guards were bribed. It happened three times. (See Wikipedia, the Internet encyclopedia and click on The Great Wall of China link.}

The One-Eyed King and His Enemies

Fast forward to 1025 BC. Saul had been crowned the king of Israel. Israel wanted a king like all the other nations. Looking at the Egyptian model of monarchical government, they felt they could resolve their political and military issues through a monarch. As indicated in the book of Samuel, this desire for a king was in complete opposition to God's wishes. But, in the end, God gave them their wish. Be careful what you wish for. You just might get it.

The enemy within the man is just as formidable as the enemy he fights on the battlefield.

Israel got their king. But as we know from Old Testament history he was a king who wrestled with his own personal demons, as most kings do. The nation of Israel was constantly confronted with these five warring tribes, distant relatives bent on their destruction. Now we will focus all of that history on one man and the struggle he had with his five enemies. We will recognize that the enemy within the man is just as formidable as the enemy he fights on the battlefield. I've been told of an African proverb that says when there is no enemy within, the enemies outside cannot hurt you. It is the enemy in our heart that poses the greatest threat to our success.

Saul started out on a good path. Saul, his army, and a miracle from God defeated the Philistines in their first battle. He went on to defeat Moab, Ammon, Edom, the kings of Zobah, and the Amalekites. But lurking within his heart were some perilous factors that were never resolved. These seeds of unresolved conflict would grow into weeds that would overtake the garden of his life and eventually bring him down. Outwardly, Saul possessed all the qualities needed to become a great king. But, inwardly, he could never conquer these enemies.

The Enemy of Disobedience

Samuel also said unto Saul, The LORD sent me to anoint thee to be king over his people, over Israel: now therefore hearken thou unto the voice of the words of the LORD. Thus saith the LORD of hosts, I remember that which Amalek did to Israel,

*how he laid wait for him in the way, when he came up from
Egypt. Now go and smite Amalek, and utterly destroy all that
they have, and spare them not; but slay both man and woman,
infant and suckling, ox and sheep, camel and ass.*

—1 Samuel 15:1-3

"I remember what Amalek did to Israel." God does not forget
history. He remembers. That's why it is so important that we do too.
What did Amalek do? When the Israelites came out of Egypt the
Amalekites ambushed the rear of the Israelites, attacking the slow
folk: the women and the elderly. They were a cowardly bunch and
God did not forget their treachery. So, God told Saul to rise up and
fight the Amalekites and destroy them—all of the people and all of
their possessions.

*And Saul smote the Amalekites from Havilah until thou
comest to Shur, that is over against Egypt. And he took Agag the
king of the Amalekites alive, and utterly destroyed all the people
with the edge of the sword. But Saul and the people spared Agag,
and the best of the sheep, and of the oxen, and of the fatlings,
and the lambs, and all that was good, and would not utterly
destroy them: but every thing that was vile and refuse, that they
destroyed utterly.*

—1 Samuel 15:7-9

Saul made a tragic mistake and his disobedience became the
roots for his failures. If you spare your enemy, your enemy will kill
you. God did not curse him. He cursed himself. God did not take
Saul down. He took himself down. He was his own worst enemy.
What a surprise. Disobedience was his enemy. He chose to disobey
God's Word and his disobedience brought him down.

> *For rebellion is as the sin of witchcraft, and stubbornness is*
> *as iniquity and idolatry. Because thou hast rejected the word of*
> *the* Lord, *he hath also rejected thee from being king.*
> —1 Samuel 15:23

Rebellion is the sin of witchcraft. Witchcraft is the decision to listen to *other* voices rather than the *divine* voice. Rebellion and disobedience fall in the same trap as witchcraft. It is the determination to choose your path rather than the path God has ordained for you. It is the resolve to reject His will and seek your own destiny. Leaders who choose the way of self over the way of God will fall into the snare of their own destruction—self-made destruction. They fall under the illusion that they know better than God.

Obedience is better than sacrifice. Not all sacrifices are the same. There are some sacrifices that get us into trouble. When God's will is in conflict with our will, the decision we make at that moment will determine our future.

David was a different kind of one-eyed king than Saul. David was a praying person. Have you ever noticed any discussion in the Bible about Saul praying? Not very much! David sought God's will while Saul sought his own counsel.

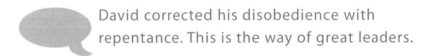

David corrected his disobedience with repentance. This is the way of great leaders.

We must become people of the divine *yes.* Those people with a *yes* in their spirit will succeed in life. I don't give no for an answer, and I don't take no for an answer. When you allow your life to make harmony with God's will you can destroy your enemies. You might make mistakes but when confronted with the right way, you respond with a "yes." In 2 Samuel 12, we find the account of the prophet Nathan, who was Samuel's successor as public servant and spokesman of God, having the unenviable responsibility of opposing David regarding his adulterous affair with Bathsheba and his subsequent murder of her husband, Uriah. When Nathan stuck his boney finger in David's face, what did David do? Confronted with his sin, rather than killing himself, he repented. He corrected his disobedience with repentance. This is the way of great leaders.

It's like the kid whose mother gave him two nickels for Sunday school. One was for the offering and one for a treat. On his way there he dropped one of the nickels in the sewer and said, "Oops, there goes the Lord's nickel!" It is easy to give God the leftovers of our lives. It is easy to walk the way of partial obedience. But great leaders are those who are willing to obey God at all cost.

The Enemy of Arrogance

> *And Samuel came to Saul: and Saul said unto him, Blessed be thou of the Lord: I have performed the commandment of the Lord. And Samuel said, What meaneth then this bleating of the sheep in mine ears, and the lowing of the oxen which I hear? And Saul said, **They** have brought them from the Amalekites: **for the people** spared the best of the sheep and of the oxen, to sacrifice unto the Lord thy God; and the rest we have utterly destroyed.*
>
> —1 Samuel 15:13-15 (emphasis added)

Saul greeted Samuel with covert arrogance suggesting that he had completely followed the direction of Samuel. Saul forgot that Samuel was a prophet. Prophets know. It's a real pain sometimes, but that's just how it works. So Samuel pushed the issue further and asked him if that was the sound of sheep. Whose sheep were those? Saul was caught in his own lie and then blamed it on the people. It wasn't his fault. Besides, they were going to use these animals to make a sacrifice to God. Not all sacrifices are good sacrifices. We should never sacrifice that which we should have destroyed. The image of the Lord has been replaced with a mirror. He has become more concerned with his own image than God's image.

Arrogant people always think that they know a better way to do something. They think the rules do not apply to them. The way of God is the humble way, and God will exalt him. The way of man is conceit and he will bring himself down.

The Enemy of Denial

> *Wherefore then didst thou not obey the voice of the* LORD, *but didst fly upon the spoil, and didst evil in the sight of the* LORD*? And Saul said unto Samuel, Yea, I have obeyed the voice of the* LORD, *and have gone the way which the* LORD *sent me, and have brought Agag the king of Amalek, and have utterly destroyed the Amalekites.* **But the people** *took of the spoil, sheep and oxen, the chief of the things which should have been utterly destroyed, to sacrifice unto the* LORD *thy God in Gilgal.*
> —1 SAMUEL 15:19-21 (EMPHASIS ADDED)

 It is our pride that keeps us from owning up to the wrong that we have done.

When faced with his disobedience Saul attempted to deny his failure and blame it on others. It appears that he was better at justifying disobedience than executing obedience. "Men are rewarded or punished not for what they do but for how their acts are defined. That is why men are more interested in better justifying themselves than in better behaving themselves."[15]

When caught with the hand in the cookie jar, why do we find it easier to explain away our actions or blame someone else? Pride. It is our pride that keeps us from owning up to the wrong that we have done. This human behavior goes all the way back to the beginning of time in an ancient garden. When exposed by their sin, Adam and Eve invented the game of hiding and blaming. Imagine trying to hide from the One who *sees* all. Envision trying to blame others when there is One who *knows* all. It is an act of futility. With Adam and Eve we see the beginning of the language of blame shifting, rationalizations, deceptions, lies, coded language, and irresponsibility.

"And Eve originated what would become the classic copout: 'The devil made me do it.' Enter the world of recrimination, injustice, scapegoating, and irresponsibility."[16]

> *And Samuel said, Hath the LORD as great delight in burnt offerings and sacrifices, as in obeying the voice of the LORD? Behold, to obey is better than sacrifice, and to hearken than the fat of rams.*
>
> —1 SAMUEL 15:22

As I have said a number of times, there is a time to sacrifice and there is a time not to sacrifice. Not all sacrifices are created equal. Sometimes sacrifice becomes disobedience. In our way of thinking we imagine that a great sacrifice is leaving a great job or a place of influence so that we can serve God. That is a perversion of thought. When can you compare a job or a place of influence to serving God? Giving up your power as God, leaving the glories of heaven, entering the muck of man, enduring ridicule and shame, dying on a cross—that is a sacrifice!

I am dismayed at what happens with Christians over and over again. When God has called you to serve Him—anointed you and given you gifts to serve Him—and then you throw it away, this is insanity. Then you double your sin by excusing it or blaming others. Hiding and blaming are great enemies that confront us every day.

The Enemy of Impenitence

Another issue that Saul dealt with is highlighted in 1 Samuel 15:24-26:

> And Saul said unto Samuel, I have sinned: for I have transgressed the commandment of the LORD, and thy words: because I feared the people, and obeyed their voice. Now therefore, I pray thee, pardon my sin, and turn again with me, that I may worship the LORD. And Samuel said unto Saul, I will not return with thee: for thou hast rejected the word of the LORD, and the LORD hath rejected thee from being king over Israel.

In the face of his failure Saul could not get to the place where he truly repented. The words sounded good but they were disguised with the same kind of excuse-making. He could not find it within himself to fall down and repent from his heart. He just couldn't get it. His words were empty and the prophet knew it. He was given opportunity after opportunity to repent like David. He was given his chance. He was given his opportunity. But he remained unrepentant. He feared the people. Confronted by the prophet, David made no excuse. He simply said, "I have sinned."

Charles Finney (1792-1875) was a fiery New York preacher who was born in Connecticut. He never attended college, but his six foot three-inch stature, piercing eyes, musical skill, and leadership abilities gained him notoriety in his community. He studied as an apprentice to a lawyer, but following a dramatic conversion experience in Adams, New York at the age of 29, Finney became a minister and moved to New York City in 1832, where he pastored the Free Presbyterian Chatham Street Chapel and later founded and pastored the Broadway Tabernacle, known today as Broadway United Church of Christ. His presentation of the gospel message reached thousands and influenced many communities.

In 1846 he preached a sermon with the ominous title, *The Nature of Impenitence and the Measure of Its Guilt.* In the introduction to the sermon Finney made it clear that impenitence is not simply refusing to repent. It is greater than the negation of repentance. Finney declared that impenitence is more than a non-act. He called it a state of self-seeking. When men make themselves and what is supposedly good for them the object of supreme regard, this is impenitence. Finney continued by saying that if everything does not terminate in self they feel no interest in it. *To their own gratification, and their own supposed interests, they are supremely devoted.*[17]

Saul was more concerned about saving face as opposed to repenting and changing the course of his life. One of the great problems for Christians is that we know the right words—we know the "language"—but too often they are hollow words coming from an empty heart.

The Enemy of Egotism

This segues into the final enemy of our soul—egotism. At the heart of all that Saul did was an egotistical heart.

> *Then he said, I have sinned: yet honour me now, I pray thee,*
> *before the elders of my people, and before Israel, and turn again*
> *with me, that I may worship the LORD thy God.*
> —1 SAMUEL 15:30

 The more you cover up, the more you have to cover up.

What was Saul really trying to say? "Samuel, walk out with me one more time in front of the people and make it look like I am okay." Saul was embarrassed by his actions, but the only thing he wanted to do was *save face.* Attempts at saving face get a lot of people into serious trouble. What they don't understand is that this only leads to more trouble. The more you cover up, the more you have to cover up.

Saul's ego was so big and his egotism was so strong that it did not allow him to stand in front of the people and admit that he was wrong. He did not understand that the appropriate way out of his dilemma was to simply repent before God and confess his sin before the people. God would have forgiven him, and the people would have accepted him. But his actions of denial and his arrogant attempts to put on a show only made his sin worse.

Image is everything. That is the slogan in a capitalistic society bent on selling its latest product. That product can be merchandise or people. We are told that if you want to keep your career moving ahead, managing your image is a must. Your effectiveness as a leader is directly linked to how others perceive you. It doesn't matter if the perception is correct. In a world where branding and image rule the business and political world, the church has been seduced into accepting this slogan. Image is everything in the pulpit, even if you are cheating on your wife or abusing your children. The church has tried to remake its *image* into a humanistic reflection. In order to perpetuate this image we are forced to *hide* our sin and failure.

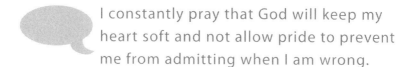

> I constantly pray that God will keep my heart soft and not allow pride to prevent me from admitting when I am wrong.

Arrogance keeps us from recognizing and admitting our sins. I have learned that image is not everything. It is more important to recognize when I have failed, and not hide it. I constantly pray that God will keep my heart soft and not allow pride to prevent me from admitting when I am wrong.

Ego is a huge problem. It is the attention to self-gratification and self-preservation. Ego places more emphasis on position, rather than the presence of God. Saul loved the position, and he used his position to promote and preserve himself. He was more interested in who he was than who God is. This is why it never bothered Saul that Israel had lost the ark in a battle with their arch nemesis, the Philistines. After a cursed period of seven months in the hands of the Philistines, the ark of the covenant finally ended up at the house of Abinadab and remained there for about twenty years (see 1 Samuel 6:1 and 1 Samuel 7:1-2).

In 1 Chronicles 13:3 we read,

> *And let us bring again the ark of our God to us: for we enquired not at it in the days of Saul.*

Saul never went after the ark because he knew that if he brought the ark back to Jerusalem, the people would worship God and he wanted the people to worship him.

One of the first things that David did when he became king was to bring back the ark. Saul was afraid that the presence of the ark would expose his arrogance and false image. Arrogance, denial, and ego prevent us from experiencing the real presence of God. In our arrogance and attempts to create an image, we substitute *emotion* for the presence of God. A skilled orator can excite the people with his enthusiastic rhetoric. Do not confuse this with the presence of God. It doesn't matter how high you can jump. What matters is how straight you can walk!

A Tragic End to a Promising Life

Then said Samuel, Bring ye hither to me Agag the king of the Amalekites. And Agag came unto him delicately. And Agag said, Surely the bitterness of death is past. And Samuel said, As thy sword hath made women childless, so shall thy mother be childless among women. And Samuel hewed Agag in pieces before the LORD in Gilgal. Then Samuel went to Ramah; and Saul went up to his house to Gibeah of Saul. And Samuel came no more to see Saul until the day of his death: nevertheless Samuel mourned for Saul: and the LORD repented that he had made Saul king over Israel.

—1 SAMUEL 15:32-35

Samuel did what Saul should have done. After the confrontation with Saul, Samuel turned his face toward Agag, who didn't like the look in Samuel's eyes. In an effort to preserve his life, he basically said, "Let bygones be bygones." Samuel was not thwarted by Agag's attempts at reconciliation. This was a time to make things right and Samuel took a sword and cut Agag into pieces.

Because Saul did not cut off the head of his enemy, his enemy would cut off his head. In 1 Chronicles 10:9 we read that after Saul committed suicide, the Philistines came upon his body and took off his head. What a tragic end to such a talented life. Saul had everything it took to be a great king. But he squandered his opportunity and in the end his life ended in catastrophe.

In 2 Samuel 1 we read about an encounter that fills in some of the details left out in Chronicles. When David returned from destroying the Amalekites he returned to Ziklag. While he was at Ziklag a man came from the camp of Saul. In the presence of David he reported about the death of Saul, but he gave us a few more facts. He reported to David that the Philistines had defeated Israel and Saul and all of his sons were now dead. David asked him if he was sure. The young man told David that it just so happened that while he was at Mount Gilboa, he saw Saul leaning on his sword.

 What you allow to remain in your life that should not be there will eventually end your life.

The man from Saul's camp told David that when Saul saw him, Saul asked him to slay him. He finished his story to David by telling him that he slew him. Then, he took the crown that was on Saul's head and the bracelet that was on his arm, and brought them to David. Stunned, David looked at him and asked him who he was. He told David that *he was an Amalekite.* (See 2 Samuel 1:8).

God had commanded Saul to destroy all of the Amalekites. The very thing Saul was commanded to destroy was the thing that destroyed him. Here is a final truth. What you allow to remain in your life that should not be there will eventually end your life. Saul decided not to deal with his issues, and in the end, his issues destroyed him. Saul was surrounded by darkness, not because the light was not shining, but because he refused to look to the light.

If you want God to use you, you must be willing to deal with your issues from within. Know your enemy. Confront your failure. Remain humble. Obey God. Fear no man. Fear God only.

5

THE PROCESS
THAT PRECEDES
THE PRESSURE

*A man does what he must—in spite of
personal consequences, in spite of obstacles
and dangers and pressures—and that
is the basis of all human morality.*[18]

ERNEST HEMINGWAY ONCE SAID that courage is grace under pressure. Greatness is born under pressure, but it is not the pressures of life that develop our character—they merely reveal it. What we do when challenges are presented to us will uncover what is in us.

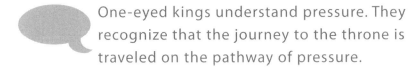

One-eyed kings understand pressure. They recognize that the journey to the throne is traveled on the pathway of pressure.

Life is not lived in a vacuum. It is filled with trials, tragedies, difficulties and challenges. But good things can emerge out of those pressures. This truth is revealed in our experiences and in nature. In the environment of pressure a life is formed. Before a child is born it must pass through the darkness and pressure of the birth canal. Under pressure pearls and diamonds are formed. And so it is with life.

One-eyed kings understand pressure. They recognize that the journey to the throne is traveled on the pathway of pressure. You cannot escape pressure. There are those who seek to escape its clutches by living their life in default and in retreat. With every challenge of life we make a decision to either allow the pressure to control us or to create us. Leaders, even the one-eyed variety, comprehend that significance is found by allowing the process of pressure to prepare you and not to break you.

I first mentioned Elijah a few chapters back. Elijah was one of the more well-known prophets of Israel. He lived in the time when King Ahab, seventh king of Israel, was in power. Ahab reigned from 871-852 BC. He became notorious not by his heroic acts, but as a result of his marriage to the evil Jezebel, daughter of the king of Tyre, a Phoenician port south of Sidon. Perhaps one of the most famous of Israel's kings, Ahab became a pioneer and champion of evil, even sponsoring Baal and Asherah worship, which had been introduced to him by Jezebel. Rituals of the Baal and Asherah cults involved detestable practices including human sacrifice of children and abhorrent sexual deviance.

This alliance was undoubtedly a means of gaining wealth for Ahab, but the unholy union eventually brought him into direct confrontation with the prophets of God, especially Elijah.

Under Jezebel's spell, Ahab led Israel down a dangerous road of treachery and defiance. She convinced Ahab to build a temple in Samaria to honor Baal. This aroused the indignation of the Jewish prophets and priests whose aim it was to purify the worship of God. Elijah stood up on behalf of God and warned Ahab that the country would suffer from drought if the cult of Baal was not removed from the land of Israel. Ahab refused, and the drought came. Don't mess with the prophet!

Elijah was not trained in a seminary for prophets. He was not even particularly qualified to handle such an intimidating match with such a ruthless ruler. But, as with all one-eyed kings, this ordinary man would accomplish extraordinary things.

Seeing, Recognizing and Understanding

In order to appreciate the value of pressure you must understand the distinction between seeing something and *recognizing* what it is and *understanding* what it does. For instance, if you do not come from a life on the streets, you would not recognize what crack is and what it does. I have lived my life on the streets. I have seen crack. I recognize what a crack vial looks like and, sadly, I understand how it destroys life.

Eighty-three percent of everything we learn comes through the eyes—what we see. Most of what we learn comes by seeing. That is why we use visual aids in our Sunday school programs. Thinking in language and words is more difficult. The best teachers know how to use these visual objects for the purpose of instruction. The picture is primary—not secondary. But it is not enough to see something. You must relate to it. You must recognize what it is you are seeing.

When I walk the streets of New York, very little misses me. I am always looking around me, and I recognize what I see. I know when a drug deal is going down. I know when a crime is about to take place. I know what girls in gaudy makeup and short skirts are saying. I recognize and understand what I see.

If you are going to survive on the streets you had better see what is going on and recognize what is happening. More than that, you had better understand what you are seeing. You have to have a point of reference for what you see. If you have never lived in this city, you will have no point of reference.

This concept also works for spiritual matters. You might see pressure coming but don't recognize why it is there. You don't understand what it can do. Your lack of understanding can and will hurt you. I am amazed at how little Bible colleges prepare young people for the pressures of life. They might know theology, but they don't know life.

Inspiration is looking at the same thing everyone else is looking at and seeing something different.

In order for us to see from a new point of reference, I have noticed that often God has to take us up a little higher. When we're stumbling around in the valley of life we can't see what is really going on. It is only when we get a little higher that we begin to understand what life is really all about. Experiences on the mountaintop help us to see, recognize and understand what life really is. Moses had to go to the top of Mt. Sinai. Elijah saw God's power on top of Mt. Carmel. Peter, James, and John saw Jesus in a different light on the Mount of Transfiguration.

In order to understand the process that precedes the pressure you have to go up to a higher plane. You cannot see life in the shallow waters of human thought. It takes divine revelation to make sense out of the craziness of things that happen in our lives. No matter how hard you try to figure it out you will fail. You must hear the voice that is bidding you to come up higher. Inspiration is looking at the same thing everyone else is looking at and seeing something different. American author, naturalist, and philosopher Henry David Thoreau (1817-1862) was right when he said that the question is not what you look at, but what you see.

I am often misunderstood because people do not understand the significance of what I see and the implications of what I do. They don't understand why I get in fights in Asia over children being sold. People don't understand my passion for the lost. When I tell you that 100,000 people go to hell every day, what does that do to you? If it does not do anything to you, then how could you ever understand the compassion that drives my life and makes me do the crazy things I do? If you really believed in hell, it should make you fall on your face because we have 4,000 people every hour of every day going there.

I don't fit in the world of preachers who drive Bentleys, live in million dollar homes, have Rolex watches and wear Armani suits. Image is not important to me. It never has been. I am more interested in reaching a world that does not know who God is.

It is clear that the church does not always see, recognize and understand the opportunities before her. Embroiled in our own theological debates and engulfed in our own selfish quests, we miss the signs of spiritual hunger all around us.

A story from history will illustrate my point. Marco Polo (1254-1324), was a famous Venetian trader and explorer who found fame from his world travels as recorded in his books. Marco Polo's father Niccolo and his uncle Maffeo were the first merchants from Venice to visit the great lands of the East. On their journey to the East, Niccolo and Maffeo Polo crossed the Volga River and finally arrived at the court of Kublai Khan (1215-1294), the grandson of the great Genghis Khan. The great Khan enthusiastically received these Europeans, the first to ever visit his court.

Kublai flooded them with a barrage of questions about the West, including questions about European rulers and the Christian religion. Kublai Khan was so captivated by the stories of Christ and the church that he asked them to return to Italy as his special messengers. He asked them to take with them a special request. They were to ask the Pope to send 100 teachers of the Christian faith to show them that the law of Christ is best. Khan promised that if he were so persuaded, he and everyone under him would become followers of Christ. What an opportunity!

After a long and arduous journey the Polo brothers finally made it back to Europe. Unfortunately, with the death of the Pope, the whole religious situation was in chaos. Arriving in their beloved Venice they ultimately were able to talk with the new Pope, Pope Gregory X, who did not offer them 100 missionaries. Instead, he assigned two, not so smart Dominican monks to return with the Polo brothers.

They left Venice in 1271 and this time they took Niccolo's seventeen-year-old son, Marco. The journey was not an easy one and soon after starting out, the monks became concerned about hazardous conditions along the route and abandoned the mission. The three Polos continued the journey, arriving at the court of the great Khan with a sample of holy oil and no trained missionaries.[19]

How many times do we have to look back in world history and ask ourselves why are we not getting this?

At the same time that he had sent the two Polo brothers to Europe, the Khan had invited the Lamas to come to Mongolia and teach them their ways. Tibet sent a wave of monks and the wave of evangelism by the Tibetan monks penetrated all of Mongolia turning them to Buddhism. As usual, what a lost opportunity!

Today sixty percent of the world population is Asian. Sixty percent! What if the church had seen, recognized, and understood the great opportunity that was offered to them by Kublai Khan? The church was given an opportunity to minister to the largest group of people in the world…to reach Christ…it was given to her on a silver platter. But they missed it! How many times do we have to look back in world history and ask ourselves why are we not getting this? How long do we have to live before we will get it right? The Pope certainly never understood the long-range historical obligations of what that one open door could have done to the largest people group in the world.

> *Now I will come unto you, when I shall pass through Macedonia: for I do pass through Macedonia. And it may be that I will abide, yea, and winter with you, that ye may bring me on my journey whithersoever I go. For I will not see you now by the way; but I trust to tarry a while with you, if the Lord permit. But I will tarry at Ephesus until Pentecost. For a great door and effectual is opened unto me, and there are many adversaries.*
> —1 CORINTHIANS 16:5-9

The apostle Paul was faced with a door of opportunity and was willing to walk through that door. It was a door of obligation but also a door of opposition as well. It was a door that opened the Gospel to the Gentiles. A whole world was introduced to Christ. I wonder if we will walk through our doors of opportunity in these times.

Not every door we walk through will be easy. We will quickly learn that doors of opportunity also have opposition on the other side. American Presbyterian leader and principal of Princeton Seminary, A. A. Hodge (1823-1886), served as a missionary to India, held pastorates at Lower West Nottingham, Maryland, Fredericksburg, Virginia, and Wilkes-Barre, Pennsylvania before accepting the call to Princeton as chair of systematic theology. He touched the religious world in many areas. Hodge seemed to feel that it was easier to find a score of men wise enough to discover the truth than to find one intrepid enough, in the face of opposition, to stand up for it. Where are those men today?

Fighting Jezebel and Her Prophets

Getting back to our boy, Elijah, this guy was not a novice. He was no intern in the school of the prophets. He was a seasoned veteran, who had experienced many challenging battles. But he was about to fight his biggest battle. First, he would confront the prophets of Baal and then Jezebel would confront him. The prophet was in for the fight of his life.

From her personal treasury, Jezebel supported 450 prophets of Baal. She went on a rampage of destruction killing the prophets of God. A showdown was building between Ahab, backed by his ungodly wife, and Elijah. Elijah invited Ahab to meet him at Mt.

Carmel. Ahab gathered the 450 prophets of Baal and sent them to Mt. Carmel.

Let the fight begin. Elijah issued his challenge.

> *Then said Elijah unto the people, I, even I only, remain a prophet of the LORD; but Baal's prophets are four hundred and fifty men. Let them therefore give us two bullocks; and let them choose one bullock for themselves, and cut it in pieces, and lay it on wood, and put no fire under: and I will dress the other bullock, and lay it on wood, and put no fire under: And call ye on the name of your gods, and I will call on the name of the LORD: and the God that answereth by fire, let him be God. And all the people answered and said, It is well spoken.*
>
> —1 KINGS 18:22-24

What a scene on the top of this historic mountain! The prophets of Baal began shouting out to their god, dancing around the altar, cutting themselves with knives, and hoping that their god would appear. Nothing.

Mocking them, Elijah suggested that maybe Baal couldn't hear them. With taunting words he told them to shout louder, that maybe Baal was busy, or had gone on a trip. As the day came to an end, bloodied and tired, they could go on no longer. Elijah now stepped up on the stage. It was God's time to show off His power.

Elijah took twelve stones, one representing each of the twelve tribes of Israel, and built an altar for the Lord. Then he dug a trench around it placing wood on top of it. Cutting a bull into pieces he arranged the body parts on the wood. Finally he poured four jars of water on the sacrifice and the wood. His helpers did this three times. And then Elijah prayed.

> *…Lord, God of Abraham, Isaac, and of Israel, let it be known this day that thou art God in Israel, and that I am thy servant, and that I have done all these things at thy word. Hear me, O Lord, hear me, that this people may know that thou art the Lord God, and that thou hast turned their heart back again.*
>
> *—1 Kings 18:36-37*

As the people watched, the tension mounted.

> *Then the fire of the Lord fell, and consumed the burnt sacrifice, and the wood, and the stones, and the dust, and licked up the water that was in the trench. And when all the people saw it, they fell on their faces: and they said, The Lord, he is the God; the Lord, he is the God.*
>
> *—1 Kings 18:38-39*

Then Elijah commanded the people to seize the prophets of Baal and kill them.

The Darkness of Depression

This was only the end of the first confrontation. Ahab ran back to Jezebel and told her all that happened, including how Elijah had all of her precious prophets killed. A furious Jezebel sent her messenger to Elijah with these words:

> *…So let the gods do to me, and more also, if I make not thy life as the life of one of them by to morrow about this time.*
>
> *—1 Kings 19:2*

Jezebel put out a contract on Elijah. He had just faced down 450 prophets of Baal. Why should he be afraid of one woman? Strangely enough, Elijah was afraid and his fear led him into a deep depression. And this is where the pressure begins. This is the process that precedes the pressure cooker.

 Depression is the scourge of this generation and has evolved over time.

I find it strange that so many men and women have faced the darkness of depression right after their greatest victories. They go from extreme highs to extreme lows.

Depression is the scourge of this generation and has evolved over time. In the past it was viewed as a simple sense of unhappiness. Now it has emerged as the curse of our times and is viewed as a psychotic disorder that requires all kinds of anti-depressants. The signs of depression are hopelessness, an inability to make decisions, lack of energy, anxiety, insomnia and dejection. It seems to be brought on by stress, a feeling of being trapped, financial troubles, an inability to handle failure, tragedy, physical ailments, and a host of other internal factors. Depression is a result of constant pressure. We are de-pressed. Something continues to press up against us, and we grow tired in resisting that pressure. Total depression is when you realize the light at the end of the tunnel is New Jersey.

Elijah had been fighting for a long time against the forces of evil. Everywhere he turned he faced the eroding work of Queen Jezebel and the prophets of Baal. In spite of a great victory, the fight became overwhelming. He had a sense (although it was a false sense) that he was the only one who was standing up to this wicked queen.

 If you do not find ways to control and manage the pressure, it will control you.

At one time or another, all of us have awakened from our restless sleep and did not want to leave our bedroom. We could not face another day. Whether the feeling was caused by dread of our work, fear of failure, or physical pain it doesn't matter. We felt trapped and hopeless. There was no light at the end of the trouble. When would this ever end? I have felt the pressure that can lead to this kind of psychological pain. The pressure of raising finances to support this work, the fear of failure, living with my own weaknesses, and the constant feeling of responsibility I have for our staff and their safety. It never goes away.

It is a process that precedes the pressure. I have learned that if you do not find ways to control and manage the pressure, it will control you. It will eat you alive. Is there a magical solution? One thing I am sure of, it cannot be totally resolved with aspirin and Prozac. Another thing I am sure of is that it is not found in the simplistic and idiotic answers Christians give to those who are in pain.

I remember once when I was in Amsterdam, I met a young widow who had just lost her husband. All I could do was ask her, "How are you holding up?" Nothing to say, is there? Nothing at all. I was not going to embarrass her or myself by offering some pretentious and religious advice. I knew the truth. That night she would go to bed alone with two kids. The funeral was over. Everyone had flown home and she was alone. In those moments, words are hollow and only God could comfort her in this excruciating pain.

Breaking the Power of Depression

Unlike Tom Cruise, I don't want to over-simplify depression. One thing I know. When you get to that place where you feel you are whipped and cannot go on any longer, then you need to do something. It is time for you to take a night…take a day…whatever it takes for you to separate yourself from the cloud of confusion. Everyone finds their own way to cope with their hopeless situations. What do I do? You might think this is crazy but it is my way. I get alone and unwind by eating a bowl of Häagen-Dazs ice cream. Now, I will probably die with clogged arteries, but I will have a great time in the process. I will die a happy man.

The key is that you need to break the pressure. Take a bike ride, go to a movie. Do something that you can control. We need to understand that we are in this thing called life for the long haul. The one who does not take a break will be broken. Living life without a pause will lead you to broken places, depressed places.

Constant fighting will lead you to constant fleeing. This is the natural response to unresolved pressure and it was the next step in Elijah's process.

God Has a Question for You

Elijah fled into the desert. While in the desert God came to him and told him that he needed to eat. One of the signs of depression is loss of appetite. The God that created us knows how to sustain us. God knew that for Elijah to get through the process that precedes the pressure, he needed the strength that comes from eating.

Depletion of energy will keep us from having the physical and mental ability to get through the process. Elijah ate and in the strength of that meal, he was able to go for forty days and ended up at Mt. Horeb. That must have been some kind of meal!

> *And he came thither unto a cave, and lodged there; and,*
> *behold, the word of the LORD came to him, and he said unto*
> *him, What doest thou here, Elijah?*
>
> —1 KINGS 19:9

The Hebrew word for "what" is *mah* and can be translated as "what or how." Both questions lead you down different roads of personal confrontation. This internal dialogue with God is key to going through the process produced by the pressure of life. Questions are powerful tools for opening up the human psyche. It is a divine tool that God has used to release man in order for him to see where he is. Questions are tools for finding the truth.

 Searching questions, shining like a brilliant flashlight, force man to inwardly confront the realities of his life.

"What are you doing here?" What do you plan to do now that you are here?" This divine inquiry opened up the question of his future. "Elijah, you are here on this mountain and now where will you go?" "What will you do?" Before Elijah could finish the process, he had to be able to answer these questions: "Why are you here?" "How did you get here?" This interrogation by God exposed Elijah to his past. "What steps have you taken to get to this place?" "Why did you flee from the presence of Jezebel?" "After the success you have had, why are you running?" "What is the source of your fear?" "How did you get from Mt. Carmel to Mt. Horeb?

Searching questions, shining like a brilliant flashlight, force man to inwardly confront the realities of his life. They compel us to examine our fear and pain—the disastrous results of our wayward actions. God has the profound ability to ask the right question at the right time. He knows what lives in the dark corners of men's hearts. Through the use of the question, God uncovers the realities of our inward lives, the lives seen by no one. But God has seen them. God sees our hearts better than we do. By the power of the query, He turns on the light in our inward parts so that we can see.

> *And he said, I have been very jealous for the LORD God of hosts: for the children of Israel have forsaken thy covenant, thrown down thine altars, and slain thy prophets with the sword; and I, even I only, am left; and they seek my life, to take it away.*
>
> —1 KINGS 19:10

 Confronting our feelings—right or wrong—is the first step to overcoming our feelings.

Now we are making progress. Elijah was opening up and revealing the source of his pain and fear. He felt like he was alone. Did you ever feel like you were all alone? Have you ever felt like no one quite understood you? I have spent probably most of my life convinced that there is not one person in this world who understands me, and am persuaded that no one really cares. Confronting our feelings—right or wrong—is the first step to overcoming our feelings.

The pressure he experienced is a pressure to perform to the level of expectation that people had of him. Elijah was fighting now. He was fleeing. He was running for his life. And God asked him,

"Why are you here?" And his answer wasn't even an answer. He was feeling sorry for himself. He felt alone. Just like you. You call 1-800-cry baby and expect somebody to answer.

> *And he said, Go forth, and stand upon the mount before the LORD. And, behold, the LORD passed by, and a great and strong wind rent the mountains, and brake in pieces the rocks before the LORD; but the LORD was not in the wind: and after the wind an earthquake; but the LORD was not in the earthquake: and after the earthquake a fire; but the LORD was not in the fire: and after the fire a still small voice.*
> —1 KINGS 19:11-12

Like the old 70s song said, sign, sign, everybody is looking for a sign. They are looking for a sign in the natural world (wind, earthquake, fire) that will give them a sense of what they should do. They are looking for some BIG event that will help them make sense of the confusion swirling around in their head. There are lots of people who chase one big meeting after another. They're looking for a sign.

What did Elijah get? He didn't get a sign. He got a *silent* voice. That was not what he was looking for. He was looking for the big miracle, the big sign. How could there be a silent voice? If it is silent then how can it be heard and understood? If you are married, you know what that is. If you know someone well enough, all you have to do is look at that person and you know what they want, need, expect, etc.

Elijah was fleeing. He did not know why he was so confused. First, he was high and now he was low. One of the great keys to life is how to manage your highs. Sometimes we get to a place of unrealistic highs based upon empty promises. Recently, a guy approached me and told me that he was going to help the ministry financially. I was very respectful and appreciative to him, but in the back of my mind I thought, he did not remember several years ago when he told me that he was going to do something and he never did. So now, he was telling me again that he was going to do this and that. I have learned not to put my hope on the promises of others. I try to avoid the high highs and the low lows. If I got high on every promise that was ever made to me I would be a psychological wreck.

> *And it was so, when Elijah heard it, that he wrapped his face in his mantle, and went out, and stood in the entering in of the cave. And, behold, there came a voice unto him, and said, What doest thou here, Elijah?*
>
> *And he said, I have been very jealous for the LORD God of hosts: because the children of Israel have forsaken thy covenant, thrown down thine altars, and slain thy prophets with the sword; and I, even I only, am left; and they seek my life, to take it away.*
>
> —1 KINGS 19:13-14

Déjà vu. God asked the same question and Elijah gave the same answer. You would think that just the *presence* of God would be enough. But sometimes you need the *voice*, not just the sense of His *presence*. You need a word, something that will help you explore the reasons for your fears and hopelessness.

> *And the LORD said unto him, Go, return on thy way to the wilderness of Damascus: and when thou comest, anoint Hazael to be king over Syria: And Jehu the son of Nimshi shalt thou anoint to be king over Israel: and Elisha the son of Shaphat of Abelmeholah shalt thou anoint to be prophet in thy room.*
>
> —1 KINGS 19:15-16

Isn't that interesting? God told him to go back to the place where he came from. Your answer to your future is often found in the past. Sometimes you have to go back and take care of the things you were fleeing. The answer to life is not in flight. It is in confronting the very things that you are afraid of. Fleeing from your fears is not the answer. The key to success is facing your fears. God apparently still had a plan for Elijah. He still wanted to use him. God told him to anoint a heathen king—a Jewish king—and a new apprentice. Then God told him that his actions would set in motion the purposes of God to eliminate the enemies of Israel.

A Frightening Situation

> *Yet I have left me seven thousand in Israel, all the knees which have not bowed unto Baal, and every mouth which hath not kissed him.*
>
> 1 KINGS 19:18

Elijah had been overwhelmed by a frightening situation that seemed larger than he felt he could stand. He felt alone. No one was there to support him. He was standing up against the tide and there was no one else who really cared. Mother Theresa once said that the greatest poverty is loneliness. Elijah's feeling of loneliness was only a feeling. It was not based on reality.

In order to break the feeling of loneliness, God revealed the real truth. And God basically said, "Hey, Elijah, you're not the only one around here who can do something! I still have 7,000 who have not bowed to Baal nor have kissed him! You are not the only one. You just think that you are. You think that you're the only one who cares. I have news for you, Pal. You are not the only one who has given up. You just think you are. So guess what? You did some good stuff. You performed some miracles. But you never understood that I have more servants than you, and you never really understood how I operate."

God had a plan to get Elijah out of this frightening place. "Why don't you just go out and get an unsaved guy [Hazael] and anoint him king? Then go and get someone else [Jehu] and I will make him a king. Finally, you're going to need a partner that you can train to eventually take your place when you have reached the end of your journey."

> Once you come back to reality, God has a word for you that will unravel the confusion and eventually accomplish His purposes. Do not give up.

How was this plan going to work? Well, God used Hazael to completely destroy the entire household of Ahab. Jehu would bring down Queen Jezebel by giving the order to throw her out the window, where the dogs licked her blood (see 2 Kings 9:33-37). And, Elisha would come to perform more miracles than Elijah ever had.

God knows how to get you through the process that precedes the pressure. You are not alone in the fight. When you flee the pressure created by a frightening place, God has a question for you that will bring you back to reality. Once you come back to reality, God has a word for you that will unravel the confusion and eventually accomplish His purposes. Do not give up. You will hear the voice of the Lord and you will see the hand of God that will turn the pressure into promise if you will just press through the pressure.

6

THE PROCESS THAT PRECEDES THE PERSEVERANCE

In the realm of ideas, everything
depends on enthusiasm; in the real
world all rests on perseverance.[20]

N O GREAT THING IS ever created *suddenly*. All miraculous things come to those who wait. In order to
survive the processes of life you must have perseverance. As children we discovered that perseverance was
needed in learning to walk and in riding a bike. We didn't do

it the first time. We fell down many times before the process was complete and success came. The only place success comes before work is in the dictionary. As adults we need to revisit these truths again and again.

Sparky, a nickname inherited from a character in the comic strip, "Barney Google," grew up in Minnesota. There was nothing special about Sparky. He was the son of a German father and a Norwegian mother. His alcoholic mother and angry brothers made life difficult at home. He did not do very well in school. He failed every subject in the eighth grade. He flunked physics, Latin, algebra and English in high school.

Sparky did not stand out among his fellow students at school. He was not actually reviled; he was simply ignored. Sparky never had the courage to ask a girl out on a date. Sparky was inconsequential and afraid of rejection. In today's vernacular, Sparky was a *loser.* To those around him it appeared that he had no skills and no passion.

But to the unseeing eye he did have one gift and one love. Sparky had a passion to draw. He took great pride in his artwork. Even though he thought he had a gift, it was not recognized. He submitted some of his artwork to the yearbook editors. It was turned down. Rejection is a great recruiter for failure. But Sparky did not give up. He continued to draw. After finishing high school, he drafted a letter to Walt Disney Studios and told them about his love for drawing. They suggested that he send them some of his works. He was rejected again. In his biography he described himself as the little boy whose kite would not fly and who never succeeded at kicking a football.

 The two hardest things in life are *starting and finishing.*

Sparky transcended his failure and from the ashes of rejection he created a character that was a caricature of his own life. This character became one of the most famous cartoon characters of all time—Charlie Brown. The artist, as you have now guessed, was the infamous Charles Schulz. As the legendary American radio broadcaster for the ABC Radio Networks, Paul Harvey, would say, "And now you know the rest of the story."

Starting and Finishing

Many times I have said that the two hardest things in life are *starting and finishing*. Starting is the easiest. It is finishing that is tedious and trying. If the word *quit* is in your vocabulary, then *finishing* is not. As someone once said, "It is not how you begin the race that counts; it is how you finish the race." Juxtaposed between the start and the finish is the act of perseverance.

You need to get that truth in your head. Starting is only the first step of the journey. These two are the most difficult things in life—the toughest things that you will ever do.

The second most important decision in life is who you marry. But the next greatest challenge is *staying* married. The pressure of staying married too often swallows up the pleasure of getting married. It takes perseverance to stay married. It takes patience to work through the problems that confront those who are married.

One of the things that I have noticed about so many Christians is that they are, as we say, so heavenly minded that they are no earthly good. They are incapable of creating a balance between the practical and the spiritual. They are good at starting things but not very successful at finishing a task. In this book you have met some rather ordinary people who did extraordinary things. Their heads were not in the clouds. Their feet were firmly planted on terra firma.

They made choices that brought them to places of opportunity to experience success with God. As you will learn in this chapter, every success was preceded by a choice and every choice was followed by perseverance.

Impact or Impression, Progress or Regress

If you are going to make an *impact,* and not just an *impression,* you had better prepare yourself to persevere. What does it take to make it for the long haul? What are some of the things that precede the mindset of perseverance? How do you overcome all the cynics and enemies in your life? I have discovered that the best revenge for those who oppose us is to develop a mindset of perseverance.

I made up my mind years ago that I would get revenge on those who tried to ruin me or cause me to quit. How did I get revenge? I decided to outlast the crowd of critics. *If you sit by the river long enough, you will see your enemies float by.* You just have to sit there long enough. The best revenge that you can have on the enemy is perseverance.

In the face of failure we must not choose the path of regression.

I look at my life and know that the dumbest thing that I could ever do at this point, besides turning my back on God, is to quit. After all I have been through, all that I have seen, after all the stuff that I have weathered—all the storms I have come through—I have come too far to give up and walk away.

In the face of failure we must not choose the path of regression. We must continue to make progress in our journey. When preparing to cross the Rubicon River, Julius Caesar told his men that even then they could draw back. But he told them that once they crossed that little bridge, they must settle things with the sword. I know that if you are reading this book, you have dealt with a lot of things. But you have made some progress. Now you are faced with a bridge. A decision must be made. By God's grace you can make the right choice. You can let your perseverance become your revenge. Even if you do not see the victory in your lifetime, you must let your life become a bridge for others to cross.

The Weeping Prophet

Jeremiah was that kind of guy. He understood that the process that led to the fulfillment of God's purposes required perseverance on his part. And he understood that he might not see his dream come true in his lifetime.

> *Is it nothing to you, all ye that pass by? behold, and see if there be any sorrow like unto my sorrow, which is done unto me, wherewith the LORD hath afflicted me in the day of his fierce anger. From above hath he sent fire into my bones, and it prevaileth against them: he hath spread a net for my feet, he hath turned me back: he hath made me desolate and faint all the day. The yoke of my transgressions is bound by his hand: they are wreathed, and come up upon my neck: he hath made my strength to fall, the LORD hath delivered me into their hands, from whom I am not able to rise up. The LORD hath trodden under foot all my mighty men in the midst of me: he hath called an assembly against me to crush my young men: the LORD hath trodden the virgin, the daughter of Judah, as in a winepress. For these things I weep; mine eye, mine eye runneth*

down with water, because the comforter that should relieve
my soul is far from me: my children are desolate, because the
enemy prevailed.
—LAMENTATIONS 1:12-16

The book of Lamentations is a follow-up of the dark sequel to Jeremiah's first book. It is not a very inspirational book. In fact, as you know, it is a downright dismal book in my opinion. The overall tone of the book is gloomy. By the time that Jeremiah wrote this book, Jerusalem and its glorious temple had been destroyed. The dynasty of David had been terminated, and the people were marching into exile. The sins of the people brought on what seemed to be irrevocable destruction. It now appeared that the covenant promises of God had been voided. But amidst all this gloom, a glimmer of hope still remained. The poet is weighed down by God's terrible judgments on Israel. In spite of the fact that this judgment cast a shadow over the presence of God, there was still hope in God's unshakable mercy.

If you're looking for words to encourage you from the Bible, this would not be the book to read. But one who had persevered and did not give up was the same individual who wrote these words. Yes, he might have been disheartened but he never gave up.

If you've ever experienced a significant loss, Lamentations is for you. It's a beautiful, though dark book on the pain of injustice and human loss. It's filled with crushing emotions: anger, desperation, fear, loneliness, hopelessness. But in reading Lamentations, those who feel wounded may feel strangely understood. The depths of suffering, well-expressed, can bring comfort and restoration.

In the introduction to his commentary on Lamentations, Matthew Henry (1662-1714) describes Jeremiah as a very young man who had been called to the prophetic ministry about 70 years after the prophet Isaiah had passed away. He was born in the Tribe of Benjamin and had practiced and exercised his call for around 40 years with great zeal and faithfulness at a time when the nation of Israel was in rebellion against God.[21] In some theological circles, the prophet Jeremiah has been called "the weeping prophet." Why? You may know the story. For 40 years, his life…his dream…his desires…everything about him was focused on his preaching and prophesying to the nation of Israel in an attempt to get them to return to the one, true God.

His entire adult life and ministry were focused on this one thing. He honestly believed and was convinced beyond any doubt that God would honor his desires to fulfill the call on his life—to bring Israel back to God. In other words, Jeremiah believed he would see the results of his work for God. He believed his dream of salvation for Israel would be fulfilled.

When Dreams Die

Everybody has a dream. You may not verbalize it, but in your heart you have a dream, a longing that some long-held desire might happen in your lifetime. It may be a very simple desire. Like you, Jeremiah had a dream. This dream was the driving force of his life. He gave all that he had to see the fulfillment of that dream. His dream was that all of Israel would be saved from the pending judgment that was standing in wait for them if they did not repent.

He was absolutely convinced that if he would just speak the truth and remain committed to the goal, God's judgment would not fall on his beloved nation. He held on to that dream until one day it finally dawned on him that his dream—his goal to save the children of Israel from destruction—was not going to come to pass. It was not going to happen in his lifetime. With great sorrow in his heart he watched as his dream went up in flames.

He had to face the facts. Israel was not going to repent and was running face forward into judgment. It is one thing to have tragedy come after you have died. It is another thing to spend 40 years of your life with a dream and watch the death of your dream played out right before your eyes.

Lamentations, sung in the minor key, is Jeremiah's lament over the sin of Israel and their judgment. The book is written in a way that its story could be remembered. In the introduction to the *New Commentary of the Whole Bible,* the editor explains that the book was written in an alphabetical acrostic.

> *"In chapters 1, 2, and 4, each verse begins with a successive letter of the Hebrew alphabet, one verse for each of the existing twenty-two letters. The fifth chapter also has twenty-two verses, but unlike the other chapters, not all the letters of the Hebrew alphabet are used. Chapter 3 is also an acrostic, but it is arranged so that three verses begin with the same letter. Thus 3:1-3 start with Aleph, 3:4-6 with Beth, descending through the entire Hebrew alphabet. As a result, this chapter is made up of sixty-six verses. Acrostics of this sort were often written as an aid to memory; in a highly oral culture where books were few, this was important. Some have pointed out that these acrostics may also make a theological point. Just as Psalm 119, another acrostic poem, illustrates that the law should command all of our attention and desire (i.e., from A to Z), Lamentations reminded the Jews that they had sinned from A to Z, and that was why they were now lamenting Jerusalem's destruction."*[22]

Jeremiah was an old man now. His dream had turned into a nightmare. His life was not ending as he had hoped. In this Jewish book he was lamenting the tragedy of his times. It was clear now that Nebuchadnezzar was going to invade Israel and the whole nation would fall. These people would be taken into captivity. This now aging and weeping prophet was standing on the street corner with all of his shattered dreams. He knew God had directed him to do what he had done. He knew it, without question.

But it was not to be. Not only did his dream not come true, the whole calamity made Jeremiah look like a fool in front of everyone, including his peers.

We know from the book of Jeremiah that he believed God did not want him to marry—to have a wife and children. (See Jeremiah 16:2). Why? He wouldn't have been able to do what God had called him to do if he had to be concerned about raising and protecting a family. He was married to his ministry. It consumed him. It was a hard task that had been given to him.

> *Before I formed thee in the belly I knew thee; and before thou camest forth out of the womb I sanctified thee, and I ordained thee a prophet unto the nations....See, I have this day set thee over the nations and over the kingdoms, to root out, and to pull down, and to destroy, and to throw down, to build, and to plant.*
>
> —JEREMIAH 1:5, 10

He was committed to his dream—this one dream. And now Jeremiah was finally at the point when he realized Israel's deliverance from judgment wasn't going to happen. All of his warnings had been dismissed—discounted as unimportant, irrelevant, and even silly.

Dreams Die Hard

Henry David Thoreau said that dreams are the touchstones of our character. Our dreams tell us a lot about who we are. I believe everyone at some point in their life has had a dream—a vision of what they hope their future will be.

What do I want to be? What do I want to do with my life? What will I be when I'm grown up?

What did you want to do? Did you want to be a missionary? A veterinarian? A doctor? A singer? A teacher? A movie star? A lawyer? A cop? At some point, you had a dream. I think all of us—maybe for just a fleeting moment—had some type of fantasy. I have a friend whose grandson dreams of being a firefighter. He's five years old, but the excitement this kid generates when he sees a fire truck is comical. All he cares about is becoming a fireman.

In school they often ask you what you want to be when you grow up. So you start thinking about that question. In facing this question when I was young, I knew the answer. When I was younger, I had a dream. I always wanted to drive racecars. That was my thing. I took machine shop/auto shop in high school. The dream of racing cars was my motivating reason for graduating from high school. It was shop class that I loved. I spent three or four hours a day in shop classes. The day after I graduated, I went right to work. My partner in shop class and I had won the Chrysler trouble-shooting contest during our senior year in high school. It was a huge thing for all of the high schools in the southeastern part of the United States.

Chrysler would come in and sabotage a car so it would not start and then the contestants had to resolve the problem and get it running within the time frame set up in advance. My buddy and I had the top time, so it opened doors for immediate employment after graduation. Eventually, I went to Ford because they had a racing program that was in its early stages of development. I was able to buy a 1961 Ford race car, while still working in that racing program.

From the time that I owned the car until I sold it to go to Bible school, I only lost one race. I lost to a 1967 GTO by half a car length. I was so mad. I can't even begin to relate how mad I was. I hate to lose. I'm still like that. Nothing has changed my mind about hating to lose. Racing was my dream and I resisted anything standing in the way of my fulfilling that dream.

Then one Sunday morning at church, an elderly lady (she probably wasn't that old; I was just very young) came up to me and looked me in the eye and said, "You need to go to Bible school." And I said, *"Okay."* There was no big, booming voice. There was no big rah, rah…just the lady's words, "You need to go to Bible school." I sold my car and went to Bible school. Just like that! And the rest, as they say, is history. But that is what started my journey—at my home church on a Sunday morning when somebody said this is what you need to do. On that day my dream took a dramatic turn in direction.

Originally, I decided to go to Bible school for a year, and I have to admit that I hated it. It was terrible! It was truly one of the worst experiences in my life! It was during the Vietnam War, and weirdness was going on everywhere, including in the church. Too many fruitcakes were trying to get out of Vietnam. Everybody was weird—doing stuff I'd never seen before. I actually witnessed more weirdness in Bible school than I'd seen while working for Ford Motor Company! It scared me, and I considered myself to be fear-less then (I wasn't as fearless as I've become in the last 28 years in Brooklyn). It really rattled me, but I stayed with it. In spite of feeling out of place, I persevered there for four years.

In our haste to make things happen we can set ourselves up for big trouble.

I had a dream when I was young. So did you. You had ideas and aspirations. We all do. The truth is that not all dreams come true. Some have been replaced with other dreams and other ideas for our lives. Some of them have been put on the shelf or stuffed in a drawer somewhere. I've said it for years, everything is a trade-off.

When I was 24 years old, I decided that I was going to get married. Sometimes you just know things. Wherever you are in life, there are times when you are convinced that you know it all. And I just knew that I was going to get married. I was convinced that it was bound to happen. And I wanted it. I wanted to be married, so I got engaged. Through that experience I discovered another truth. In our haste to make things happen we can set ourselves up for big trouble.

It wasn't long before my fiancé decided that she just couldn't live this kind of life, and I started to feel that the ministry was not going to be her cup of tea, as they say. She wanted the American dream— the house, the picket fence, two and a half kids, the cat—you know, the whole "Ozzie and Harriet" deal. She wanted a *normal* life, what- ever that is.

It would have been easier for me to go down the *normal* path of life, because it does have its appeal. It would have been better to go with the flow. Here is the challenge. The more you get into a situa- tion or a relationship, the more you are willing to give up a little of this to get a little more of that. It became more increasingly difficult to balance what I wanted and what she wanted.

I remember the night she came in and gave me the ring back. I was crushed. I was really crushed. It was the end of a dream of us serving

God together. I am here as a testimony that sometimes dreams must change—they have to be altered or replaced. Sometimes childhood dreams do become adult realities, but most do not. Most of those dreams that you have as a child fade into oblivion.

Most people enter into the dream of marriage with the expectation that the marriage will last forever. They are committed to not becoming a divorce statistic. They don't think their lives will fall apart. There are times when things just don't work out the way we hope. Sometimes, it is just a bad match. It is tragic when it happens. It can be devastating when a dream dies.

I have seen people who believed God that they would be healed. They were in every prayer line and believed every preacher on the airwaves. They accepted the promise that if they sent a $100 to the preacher on TV, God would answer their prayer. Oh, the tragedy of trusting in the words of men! Thank God, there are some who do get healed. I believe in healing. But here is what I have discovered. Not everybody who receives prayer for healing gets healed. That may shock you. I have seen it long enough. Some people die without the healing they longed for. Now we can theorize and theologize on the reasons but it is just a fact. It is a sad fact that some dreams do die.

Oral Roberts and I were talking after a meeting and I asked him, "Dr. Roberts, why doesn't everyone we pray for get healed?" I was waiting for the revelation because you know, if anybody knows the answer to that question, it would be Oral. You know what he said? "I don't know!" That was very encouraging to me.

 You have to be careful that your dreams are not fantasies.

Jeremiah knew how you feel. He had a dream for Israel, and he went to his death watching his dreams burn up in judgment. What do you do when your dream falls apart?

I was 24 when that relationship changed the course of my life. It was a very painful thing for me. I came to New York City at 31 years of age. I thought I would stay in the city for a year. I was only going to spend a year here—that was more than 28 years ago. One year turned into 28, and that is fine, but those first nine years were hell. You have no idea. You have to be careful that your dreams are not fantasies. You have a big dream that someday you will be a great person of God. You imagine all the joy that place of success will bring you. What you don't know as a young person is that greatness and success can be illusive and challenging. You have no clue what you will walk through in search of that dream.

Ministry has always been bodies and dollars. I have spent my life traveling from one city to the next trying to fund this dream. I have logged hundreds of thousands of miles in national and international flights. Flying from city to city, waiting in airports, living out of my suitcase in hotel rooms, preaching in one place after another—all of this takes its toll on the body. Traveling loses its glamour real quick. I had a dream that one day I would not have to travel as much. I would be able to slow down a bit. But here I am. I am still traveling as much as ever.

Before I knew it life had passed me by, it seemed. Twenty-eight years and I am still rushing to airports. I'm still traveling. If I don't raise the money, the buses don't run. It's pretty simple. What do you do? There are times when I become so overwhelmed at the task before me. I'll never forget when, one Saturday night, I was walking down the jet bridge at LaGuardia to go one more time, and it hit me. I can tell you exactly where it was. I was halfway down that jet bridge and the truth smacked me in the face. It will never change. I will be doing this until I die. I broke down into tears, turned around and walked halfway back home from LaGuardia. I simply could not get on that plane. I just could not do it. I turned around and started walking back home. I was crying so hard. I could not take another step. Finally, I just sat down by the side of Brooklyn-Queens Expressway and cried.

The realization came—my life will not change. This is what I will always be doing. I will always be driving to and from an airport someplace in the world, because the world will not come to where I am. And now at 60 years old, I am realizing that any hope I had of normalcy is gone.

When you face that moment, there is only one thing you can do. You cannot give up. You have to get up and keep going. You cannot turn back. Although there are many tempting parking spaces along your journey, you simply must forge ahead. You now understand that there is nothing that you can turn back to. You must persevere through the pain and heartache in the attempt to see the dream come true. Others have done it, and you can too. Let me give you an example.

A London-born man named John Newton wrote a song that most all Christians know by heart. We sing, "Amazing grace, how sweet the sound, that saved a wretch like me," but we don't feel like wretches when we sing it. John Newton did. The only child of a respected sea-captain father, he was dedicated to the Christian ministry at an early age by his devout mother. By age 4, he could recite passages from the children's hymns of Isaac Watts. At 11 he was sailing the Mediterranean with his father, but at 17 he abandoned his Christian upbringing and laid aside every religious principle he had learned. He deserted his ship, got caught and became a common felon.

His punishment was so severe that he plotted suicide. Following prison time, he lived for a while among Sierra Leone's cruel slavers. After enduring nearly constant suffering and humiliation, Newton was able to return to England on a ship where a violent storm threatened to sink the vessel. He said, "I cried to the Lord with a cry like that of the ravens which yet the Lord does not disdain to hear, and I remembered Jesus whom I had so often derided." It is said that the storm suddenly broke in his soul, and the change that took place in this man became obvious to all who knew him.

During the next six years he made several voyages as a captain of his own ship, even carrying cargoes of slaves on some occasions. Not until he reached Liverpool in August of 1754, however, did he consider himself a regenerated Christian. Gradually he consecrated himself to the Lord, hoping that he might be deemed worthy of being called into His service. After two miraculous escapes from death and several years of training and study, he was appointed a minister to the Church of England in December of 1758. Six years later he went to Olney, where he was ordained a deacon and a priest. His fellowship with William Cowper resulted in the publication of their "Olney Hymns." Number 41 Book 1, contained John Newton's life-story in this form:

Amazing Grace

Amazing grace! How sweet the sound—
That saved a wretch like me!
I once was lost but now am found,
Was blind but now I see.
'Twas grace that taught my heart to fear,

And grace my fears relieved;
How precious did that grace appear
The hour I first believed!
The Lord has promised good to me,
His word my hope secures;
He will my shield and portion be
As long as life endures.
Through many dangers, toils, and snares,
I have already come;
'Tis grace hath brought me safe thus far,
And grace will lead me home.
When we've been there ten thousand years,
Bright shining as the sun,
We've no less days to sing God's praise
Than when we'd first begun.

—JOHN NEWTON

John Newton made his last move in 1779, serving two churches in London where he labored faithfully until his death at the age of 82. He wrote his own epitaph: "John Newton, Clerk, once an infidel and libertine, was, by the rich mercy of our Lord and Saviour, Jesus Christ, preserved, restored, pardoned and appointed to preach the faith he had long labored to destroy, near sixteen years at Olney in Bucks, and twenty-eight years in this Church." He added: "And I earnestly desire that no other monument and no inscription but to this purport, may be attempted for me."[23]

The Truth about Dreams

The interesting thing about Jeremiah is that, in the face of a dying dream, he never gave up. He continued to press forward even unto his death. History says that his own people stoned Jeremiah to death in Egypt. The very people that he sought to save were the ones who took his life. During my lifetime I have discovered some important truths about dreams.

1. We all have dreams that will never come to pass.

As I've said, all of us have dreams. Most of our dreams started in our childhood. Some dreams are mistaken for whimsical desire. When we grow older those dreams change and shift. Some dreams are real but what we don't realize is that what we start today is not necessarily finished tomorrow. The fulfillment of our dream might be for another generation. Then, there are dreams that are just taken from us. You are convinced that it will never die, but you will wake up one day and realize that it is not going to go the way that you thought it would. It will not be fulfilled. I remember specifically three conversations I had with three different people that illustrate my point.

The pastor's wife that I mentioned earlier was convinced that she and her husband would grow old together, raise their children, and serve the Lord together. He died. Her dream of their future died with him. Forty-seven years old, and she said, "I was sure that we would grow old together."

I remember my conversation with a pastor who said, "I thought I would be in the ministry all of my life." But something happened that made it necessary for him to step down. He is now working construction for homebuilders.

The third person was a missionary for 25 years. His dream was to see his kids grow up and take over the work that he had begun. I think that most men have that dream. You just naturally hope your children will be interested in what you have built over their lifetime.

This man had a dream. He said, "I thought that my kids would take it over." He gave everything he had on the field, but a short time ago, a couple of the board members rose up and split the work—totally ripping it apart. They are now suing the church. He just had to send his kids back to the United States, because one of them is having a nervous breakdown.

His children saw their father give his life to this work only to see other people—people they thought were friends and supporters of their father—tear it all apart. These men not only destroyed the church, but they destroyed this family as well. The son said, "If this is ministry, I don't want anything to do with it!" I have spent too many years watching lives being destroyed and watching people throw their lives (and the lives of others) away because of their own choices.

2.   You are a part of someone else's dream.

A lady who was once on staff here at Metro Ministries recently told me that she never realized what she had when she was here. How many times have I heard that? She never realized what she had at Metro that was so precious and wonderful. She never realized that there are literally hundreds of people who wish that they could be here. Every year, many thousands of dollars are spent on airplane tickets and on hotels for people who come here to visit—*sometimes for only one day.* Thousands call and say it is their dream to come and just ride one of our Sunday school buses.

Recently, I spoke with a girl who said it was her lifelong dream to come here and ride the buses with us just once. There are people whose lives will be fulfilled by making a commitment to the dream of another. There are people who have made tremendous sacrifices to come here for a week. They have become a part of my dream and in the end my dream has become their dream.

No man is an island. We are all impacted by the dreams of others and sometimes their dreams become our own.

When I hit 50 I remember thinking, "This is it!" "This is my life." Some time ago, I collapsed in a hotel room. I completely blacked out and woke up on the floor. Just boom! I was standing in front of the mirror and the next thing that I remember, I was on the floor. Has it come to this? I began to consider my life—all the travel, all the pressure, all the responsibility and all the sacrifices. I was like a baseball player, committed to his team and playing through all his pain. They are no different. It's what they do. It's what they love. And it hit me—this is what I do. I know that the average young preacher thinks that he or she would love to do what I do. They think they have identified their life's dream—to be able to travel all around the world and have a huge ministry.

In many ways we are all a part of the dreams of others. No man is an island. We are all impacted by the dreams of others and sometimes their dreams become our own. There are those who have gone before us who have paid a price so that others could enjoy their dreams. Martin Luther King had a dream and in many ways he was not able to see that dream come true. But others now enjoy many of the things he dreamed of. Jesus had a dream for God's people. He went to the cross and died for His dream. His disciples were able to see that dream come true.

3. Life is about helping others make their dreams come true.

I have come to realize that one of the great joys of my life is to help other people discover and realize their dreams. That is pretty much how I have spent my life. I want to help others to achieve their dreams.

Out of the pain, impoverishment and isolation of my own abandonment, I have developed a heart of compassion for suffering children everywhere. From the ghettos of America to the garbage dumps of Manila to the sexual slave trade in Southeast Asia, I have sought to rescue hurting children, offering a message of love and hope while combating issues like hunger, poverty, child prostitution and AIDS. Why do I do this? I want them to have a dream. I want these precious children to be able to fulfill their dreams of rising out of their own pain and fulfilling their destiny.

Each year, we seek to provide hope and support to inner city families during the holidays. Each Thanksgiving, we operate a program called "Boxes of Love," which provides a 25-pound box of food and a turkey to the desperately needy in the community.

So many children in the inner city feel the impact of poverty on a daily basis. This is especially true at Christmas time when many parents cannot afford to provide gifts to their children. Young children often don't understand this and interpret their lack of gifts as an indication that they are not loved or not special enough to receive a gift on Christmas.

Each year Metro operates a program called "Operation Holiday Hope," which provides toys or food or shoes to needy inner-city children, many of whom would not receive gifts of any kind for Christmas. In 2007, with the help of its supporters, Metro was able to give away 81,000 toys. They come for a simple present…the excitement of ripping the paper off to see what's inside…perhaps a doll or a truck or a video game. We are glad they like the gifts, but we give the presents so they will hear the Christmas story. People are more open to the Gospel at Christmas than at any other time of the year. Those 81,000 smiles mean that 81,000 children were given the opportunity to receive Jesus into their heart. They come for a present, but they learn about the greatest gift ever given. I have a dream that these kids will be able to some day have their own dreams.

So, here I am. I keep traveling. I keep preaching. I keep raising money and awareness so that young people can come to Metro Ministries around the world and fulfill their own dreams of serving God. I want to give them the freedom, resources and ability to serve God in a new way. I am here to help them fulfill their dreams. That is why I do what I do. I may not have realized all of my dreams, but I am going to do everything I can to give these young people the opportunity to realize their dreams.

What has God planned for you? What kind of dreams does He dream for you? What kind of dreams do you have for serving God? What is in you? It is my prayer that in some way I might be able to help people find what is in them and bring it to pass. Again, this is why I do the things I do—to provide a place where others can enjoy serving God by serving these young valued lives.

You will have a dream and you may not ever realize your dream. Whatever category your dream is in, it may not happen. But realize that right now you are living someone else's dream. And you may not understand this truth, but you need to. Why don't you just decide that you are going to help someone else live their dream? That is why I keep running the buses, walking the streets, and providing the gifts. I want to be a bridge for others to cross in search of their dreams.

I realize now that some of my dreams will never come to pass. But if the Bible is true, you need that dream…that focus on life. But remember that those things you thought you were going to get may not materialize. It is okay. You can help someone else get their dreams. You can be a part of someone else's vision for the future. I cannot think of a greater joy than the joy that comes from helping another walk into their future and discover their dream.

THE PROCESS
THAT PRECEDES
THE PRICE TAG

Life is not easy for any of us. But what of that? We must have perseverance and above all confidence in ourselves. We must believe that we are gifted for something, and that this thing, at whatever cost, must be attained.[24]

EVERYTHING IN LIFE HAS a price tag, a cost attached to it. There's a credit card called MasterCard. That's why it's called *master* card. It becomes your master. If you want to accomplish something in life, as I've said, there is always a trade-off. In order to grab hold of the future, you have to let go of the past. This is a principle of life and those who are afraid to let go of their secure place will never be able to find the future that awaits them. You cannot have it both ways. If you want to serve God, that's great. But with service comes sacrifice. I have met many people in my life who want to go into ministry. They want to serve God, but they cannot let go of all the things they have accumulated in life. They are anxious about the possibility of financial security and public criticism. They want the glory but they don't want to pay the price for the glory.

 Life always presents to us challenges that will either take us to the next level or bring us down.

If you can't cut it and if you do not have the discipline then you might as well stop right now. Your hesitancy should not be about whether you can hack it or not. In my opinion there is no challenge or temptation that is insurmountable. The Bible says, *No weapon formed against me will prosper* (Isaiah 54:17). And *I can do all things through Christ who strengthens me* (Philippians 4:13). You can serve God—it's up to you to believe the Word of God—not your doubts.

But the truth still remains, there is a price tag attached to everything we do. Even those who have found their way to a successful life have made great sacrifices along the way. Life always presents to us challenges that will either take us to the next level or bring us down.

Proactive or Reactive

And God said to Noah, This [rainbow] is the token of the covenant, which I have established between me and all flesh

130

upon the earth. And the sons of Noah, that went forth of the ark, were Shem, and Ham, and Japheth: and Ham is the father of Canaan. These are the three sons of Noah: and of them was the whole earth overspread. And Noah began to be an husbandman, and he planted a vineyard; and he drank of the wine, and was drunken; and he was uncovered within his tent. And Ham, the father of Canaan, saw the nakedness of his father, and told his two brethren without. And Shem and Japheth took a garment, and laid it upon both their shoulders, and went backward, and covered the nakedness of their father; and their faces were backward, and they saw not their father's nakedness. And Noah awoke from his wine, and knew what his younger son had done unto him. And he said, Cursed be Canaan; a servant of servants shall he be unto his brethren. And he said, Blessed be the LORD *God of Shem; and Canaan shall be his servant. God shall enlarge Japheth, and he shall dwell in the tents of Shem; and Canaan shall be his servant.*

—GENESIS 9:17-27

This is one of the best known stories of all time—Noah and the ark. It took place during a time of great moral upheaval on the earth. God had done everything possible to redeem His creation. Now He was forced to take drastic action. The decline was irreversible. He would destroy the earth by a flood.

Other than those in the ark, every living creature on earth died in the flood. As the waters receded, God made a covenant with Noah that he would never destroy the earth again. The rainbow in the sky would be a sign of that covenant or promise.

After Noah and his family were finally able to land on dry ground, Noah faced his greatest test. He had just survived the greatest catastrophe of all time. He was faithful to the task given to him by God.

But after his greatest victory, he encountered his greatest defeat. Humanity was given a new covenant and a second chance. Right on the heels of that new covenant, we find Noah naked and drunk in his tent. What was he thinking? This was supposed to be a new beginning for man.

While Noah was drunk and naked in the tent, Ham sneaked in and committed some despicable and reprehensible act in that tent. His brothers were aware of their father's condition in the tent and in an effort of honor they walked backwards into the tent so as not to look upon his nudity. Slipping up to his drunken body, they covered him up. That's a whole message all by itself.

Eventually Noah awoke from his stupor and knew something had happened. He knew Ham, the younger brother, had done something. Something bad happened in the tent and Noah knew it. Because of Ham's actions he was cursed, and he would now become a servant to his brothers forever.

How is it possible that when you have won your greatest battle, when you have come through the greatest victory of your life, when you see the greatest miracles that you have ever seen, and when all of your family is saved, you fail yourself, your family and God? We saw it with Elijah, we see it again here.

 Most people react to life's situations, rather than preparing for them.

There is something to consider here. The only reason these sons of Noah were alive was because they were part of his family. They had done nothing to warrant being saved. They were just fortunate to be in the right family at the right time. They should have taken advantage of that opportunity. They should have been proactive, rather than reactive. They should have recognized their opportunity and become proactive in God's rebuilding program. They squandered their opportunity! What a surprise.

Unfortunately, I have found that most of the time the church is reactive, rather than proactive. Most people react to life's situations, rather than preparing for them. Life gets crazy, so you react. A calamity happens, and we react. Someone criticizes us; we react. Someone gets sick; we react. We don't seem to have the prophetic instincts or good sense to be proactive in a situation. We allow our emotions or our insensitivity to take charge.

I have noticed the church is normally five to seven years behind the world as far as growth and progress go. We don't do well in the face of opportunity or disaster. We are more concerned about our own little world than the world of opportunity around us. After September 11, 2001 it seemed that the church was comatose and more concerned about why this happened, rather than what they could do to help those families in New York City that had suffered.

I must say I was happy to see that the church might have learned a lesson. When Hurricane Katrina hit, it was the church that rushed to the rescue. While government agencies were trying to figure out what to do, the church was already there on the ground helping those folks who had lost literally everything. I was shocked and amazed and proud when I was in Mississippi a while ago and saw how the churches had responded.

> *By faith Noah, being warned of God of things not seen as yet, moved with fear, prepared an ark to the saving of his house; by the which he condemned the world, and became heir of the righteousness which is by faith.*
>
> —Hebrews 11:7

By faith Noah was warned by God. He didn't react negatively to God's word. He proactively responded. He moved immediately and started to build the ark and get his family ready. Unfortunately, the church today is more concerned about its new building than they are about building their community. They are focused on the inside of the church rather than the outside. Committees and programs bog the church down in a slough of frenetic activity. I find that church committees tend to be useless. My definition of a committee is very simple. They are the unfit appointed by the unwilling to do the unnecessary. Here at Metro, we do not have committees. We have teams—teams that are willing to simply jump in and do the work. We are not engaged in fruitless debate about what we should do. We see what should be done, and we do it.

 A person without principle will be a person without direction.

I teach our staff and students that we must be proactive. When there is a need we move. We recognize the urgency of opportunity and respond. We cannot whine about the problems in the church and in our world if we have not been proactively working to create solutions to those problems. God is looking for those who have eyes to see and feet that will walk. It is not enough to analyze the problem. At some point we must fix the problem.

In the life of Noah we discover five critical principles—truths that will help us face our own world. I believe in the power of a principle. There are principles that guide my life. A person without principle will be a person without direction. But it's not enough to have principles. The great people are those who consistently act upon those principles. In this book we have unlocked some key principles in the lives of the one-eyed kings. In Noah's life we will discover certain truths that will help us maximize our opportunities and minimize our defeats.

1. The Power of a Warning

God warned Noah of the impending doom. What do you do with a warning? Do you ignore it and pretend that the warning has no meaning? The *credibility* of a warning is dependent upon the character of the person giving the warning. The *probability* of the warning is dependent on the power of the person directing the warning. Many times a parent's warning to their kids lacks credibility because too often they do not follow through with their warning. God warned Noah. His character and His power back the credibility and the probability of a warning from God.

The morality of a nation is the test of a nation's character. Unfortunately, America is failing that test. Liberal theology, liberal politics and political correctness have invaded the church structure and are leading us down a dead end road that could spell our judgment. Homosexuality, adultery, sexual abuse, murder, drugs and hosts of other evils are polluting the world that we live in. There is an impending doom if we are not careful to reverse this trend.

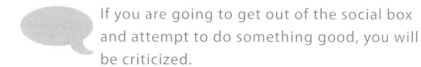

If you are going to get out of the social box and attempt to do something good, you will be criticized.

Noah built an ark on the basis of God's warning. People laughed at him, they laughed at me and, by the way, they will laugh at you too. I don't know why that bothers you. I don't know why it bothers Christians if people are critical of them. If you don't have the desire to change something you don't have the right to criticize it. If you are going to get out of the social box and attempt to do something good, you will be criticized. The world and the church have never lacked for critics. If you cannot handle criticism you will never be successful. We are now one of the ten most duplicated ministries in the world today. Nobody's laughing now!

Noah warned the people of the looming crisis. They were left without any excuse. Noah made it clear to them that a flood was coming and judgment was imminent. The people surrounding Noah looked on in scorn, laughing at his big boat. The laughing turned to terror when the rain became a deluge.

Most humans don't understand the power of a warning. We either underestimate the person issuing the warning or we foolishly think we can escape the coming cataclysm. We all think that we are tougher than we are. We just don't get it, do we? We are convinced that we have all the answers. We have it figured out. What we don't understand is that there are certain forces that are greater than we are and if you mess with them they will kill you.

2.   The Energy of Motion

While others ignored the warning, Noah heeded the warning. Noah moved. He moved his family into the boat along with the animals. He was warned and he moved. When we know what needs to be done we had better move. Too often, we are praying about what we should do, rather than doing what we know we should do. Too many people use prayer as a way to avoid responsibility. When you know what needs to be done, you don't need to pray. You don't need to put in a praise and worship tape to get in the mood. You need to act!

People often ask me what they should do in their own city. I don't have formulas. The only biblical principles that I understand are actions. There is power in moving. Motion is one of the great laws of the universe. All creation is in motion. It is easier to move an object that is in motion. But all motion causes friction. After 40 years of ministry I am convinced that the most miserable people I know are not sinners, they're Christians who know what they're supposed to be doing, but for whatever reason, just won't do it. And, they live with it every day. Start doing something, and then God can direct you.

Albert Einstein said that the world is a dangerous place, not because of those who do evil, but because of those who do nothing. Just do something. Too many in the church are more like architects than builders. We love making plans and designing strategies. You know what? Eventually, you have to put the pen down, pick up a hammer and start building something.

Before you can move the world, you must move yourself. The sedentary life is the unfulfilled life. Life is about motion. There is a time to rest and contemplate but at some point life must begin to move. In Ecclesiastes 9:10 King Solomon said, *Whatsoever thy hand findeth to do, do it with thy might.*

Too often talking is a substitute for walking. There is a time to transcend the world of words and move into action. I get frustrated when we know something is coming our way and we do nothing. When there is a pending issue coming our way we act. We must feel the sense of urgency that exists all around us. That urgency must become the motivation for our actions. I said this 30 years ago. There's been all kinds of spin-offs, but here's the original. If you want something you've never had before, you've got to do something you've never done before. This isn't rocket science, folks.

3. The Art of Preparation and Building

Noah was warned, he moved, and next he built what God told him to build. He built something. Someone once said that if they were asked what they would want most if they were shipwrecked on a lonely island, they would respond by saying that they would want the book *How to Build a Boat.* That's the kind of mental toughness I am looking for. I am not looking for philosophers. I am looking for builders.

 There is a time to pray and a time to build.

We are still in the midst of building here at Metro. We are not building something fancy. We don't have any new buildings here. What we are building won't be a $30 million dollar cathedral, because you don't need a $30 million dollar cathedral to win folks to Jesus Christ. I am shocked at the amount of money people spend on church buildings. I think how this excessive amount of money could be put into ministering to the community.

There is a time for planning and there is a time for building. Quit talking about it and start doing something about it. Stop praying. Yes, I said that. Stop praying. There is a time to pray and a time to build. We have been praying for revival. We have been praying for change…for something different to happen. It is time to quit praying and start acting upon that which God has already said. We know what needs to be done. It is time to build.

Noah was warned, he prepared, and he built. It is impossible to serve God effectively without building. Building is at the heart of God. *In the beginning God created,* according to Genesis 1:1. God *built* a world that could fulfill His dream. If you don't want to build, then stop right now.

One of the enemies of building is apathy. People still have way too much time on their hands and they waste that time in frivolous activity. Here is a truth that few people seem to understand. Once you have lost time you never get it back.

"Some day I will get around to it." Those who live their lives by that philosophy will never get around to it. Time is an illusion. We think we have more of it than we really do. The wise person will spend his time in building for the future. We used to think that time had some kind of mystical power and would heal all things. It doesn't. Martin Luther King addressed this issue of the false concept of time in his *Letters from a Birmingham City Jail.*

> *"I had also hoped that the white moderate would reject the myth concerning time in relations to the struggle for freedom. I have just received a letter from a white brother in Texas. He writes: 'All Christians know that the colored people will receive equal rights eventually, but it is possible that you are in too great a religious hurry. It has taken Christianity almost two thousand years to accomplish what it has. The teachings of Christ take time to come to earth.' Such an attitude stems from a tragic misconception of time, from the strangely irrational notion that there is something in the very flow of time that will inevitably cure all ills. Actually, time itself is neutral; it can be used either destructively or constructively. More and more I feel that the people of ill will have used time much more effectively than have the people of good will. We will have to repent in this generation not merely for the hateful words and actions of the bad people, but for the appalling silence of the good people. Human progress never rolls in on wheels of inevitability; it comes through the tireless*

efforts of men willing to be co-workers with God, and without this hard work, time itself becomes an ally of the forces of stagnation. We must use time creatively, in the knowledge that the time is always ripe to do right."[25]

You can do with that whatever you want to do with it.

 I would rather that you waste my money than waste my time.

Maybe it is because I am a little older now. But I am just a little bit more conscious of time. I wish someone would have talked to me like this when I was younger so I could have learned, but nobody did. So I had to learn it on my own. Time is valuable. I would rather that you waste my money than waste my time. I can get more money, but I can't get any more time. I am in building mode, building something that will accomplish God's purposes. I cannot allow people around me who will waste my time. My time is limited, and so is yours.

To me, the lyrics to the song, "Time in a Bottle," that American singer/songwriter Jim Croce (1943-1973) wrote in celebration of the birth of his newborn son, A.J. Croce, define the issue of the urgency of time. Due to copyright issues, I can't include them here in their entirety, but look it up on the Internet, and I'm sure you'll see what I mean.

Croce wrote of trying to save our most special moments in a time capsule that would remind us forever of the treasure of those things that are truly important: the people we love, the time we spend doing good and right things that God truly uses to bless the hearts and lives of others in His creation. Unlike most of today's music, the lyrics were meaningful and relevant. Refer to this endnote (26) at the back of the book and find the words for yourself.[26]

Croce couldn't have known that his life would be so brief. He died in a small commercial plane crash on September 20, 1973 at the age of 30. That young man accomplished much in a very short period of time. How we spend the time we are given is extremely important. There is very little in life that is more valuable than the time God has given us to accomplish all that He has directed us to do.

Noah moved after he was warned, and he was told to build something. What are you building? If you are building, build something that is going to last. And time is of the essence. We cannot wait for another generation to do what we should be doing.

I am trying to build something that will be here when I am gone. I am trying to build something so that the next generation can come and be blessed and be ministered to. I am planting trees under which I will never sit.

Matthew 16:18 records Jesus telling His disciples that upon this Rock, He would build His church. Jesus was a builder. His building program in the lives of twelve men constructed a community of people that revolutionized their world!

When I came to New York City, I wanted to build something that made no sense. I want you to build something that is so foolish it makes no sense to all those religious folk. But they will understand it later. That is what happened here. Nobody got it. It made no sense whatsoever. But it made sense to me. I had seen the future and I built upon that vision. Now they get it. Well, some have.

People thought I was crazy and they criticized me. But I was not building for that audience. I was building for children and young people who had no hope. I was building a place of hope for them. I want to build something like Noah, something that will not sink in the middle of a storm. I know that when you build according to the Word of God it will resist all storms. It will last forever!

I read in a Christian magazine article that *Focus on the Family* noted in 1998 that "about 1,500 pastors are quitting the ministry every month." Four thousand churches opened and every year seven thousand closed. How can this be? What will cause the extinction of ministers and ministries? The article cited reasons that include moral failures, spiritual burnout, or contention in their churches. The magazine interviewed pastors who were not headline-making leaders who said "they're still following Christ, they're just not getting paid for it anymore. Some left just in time to avoid ministry burnout. Some waited too long. Others reached the conclusion that God has called everyone to ministry, and they can serve in other ways."[27]

 The writers of the Bible understood that we are strengthened in our trials, not beaten.

It is my opinion that we have become too soft. We just don't have it. We have forgotten our roots. We are unaware of the divine power that is at our disposal. We have lost our moral compass and our internal fortitude.

The enemy comes against folks who are doing something. I don't know why some people are shocked when they encounter conflict. Do not get shocked. Trials and troubles are a part of our walk with God. The writers of the Bible understood that we are strengthened in our trials, not beaten.

Some were shocked when I was shot a few years ago. I wasn't. I know when you attempt to build something right there will be those who oppose you. Nothing good comes without opposition and criticism. It is the nature of life among humans.

When you make up your mind that you will not quit then there is nothing that can stop you. The storm will test the stability of what you have built. I am not interested in how many Bible verses you have memorized or how many times you have fasted. I am not impressed with what Bible college you went to or how often you pray. Just tell me this one thing. How are you when the storms of life roll onto the shores of your life? If you are still floating after the storm hits you then I will be impressed.

Noah and his family were in the ark and it was one stinking place. The smell, the sweat, and the body waste (there were no toilets or porta-potties) filled the air. What a stinking environment! But they were afloat. The critics and the scoffers were all gone. They had survived the storm of the century. They were not drowning. Noah had built something that could survive the Flood.

I might need to remind you that there is no safety in the stock market or your retirement fund. There is no safety in your looks or your personality. There is no safety in your job or your bank account. All of these things can disappear. Noah built a boat and some say that it is still there on Mt. Ararat, in the far east of Turkey close to the borders of Iran, Iraq and Armenia. He built a boat that could last through the most violent storm of all times.

Education is important but education does not guarantee that you can survive a deluge of difficulty in your life. It is good to have financial security but your money won't help you when your world collapses in on you. The tests of life are not in the classroom; they are in the valleys and deserts—always have been.

Eventually you will find rest on the mountain. Noah and his family found their mountain after their test. There is a mountain for all who are builders. After God worked for six days He rested. After Jesus died He found His mountain of resurrection. After every test there are new levels. When it is all over and you get through the storm, you are now at a new level. You are seated at this brand new level. You are sitting on the mountain. You've gone through the storm, you have endured the flood and you are now sitting on top of the mountain. The storm has made you stronger and wiser. You have learned some things in the midst of the storm. Some powerful truths have been built into your life.

 With every new level you encounter new challenges.

But there is no final rest until life is over. With every new level you encounter new challenges. *New heights bring different fights.* The longer you live, the more battles you go through and the more testing you will have to endure. Every new victory will bring a new enemy. I don't deal with the same stuff I dealt with at the start of this ministry or when I was 20 years old.

I passed those classes of crisis and now I am in a new grade with new adversity to confront. I am in a different class than the young people on my staff. They have their struggles—struggles that I faced many years ago. Now my struggles are much different than theirs. All of us who desire to build something permanent for God will go through the tests of life. As we graduate we move on to other ordeals.

You may be right in the middle of a battle right now. Perhaps you are wondering where all this adversity is coming from. You thought that when you made up your mind to serve God there would be no other tests. That is an old lie. Life is a battle. You are engaged in a battle that you never expected and fighting people you never expected to fight. That's the bad news. The good news is that you are not alone and that "no weapon formed against you will prosper" (see Isaiah 54:17). You don't get strength for the battle, you get strength from the battle.

There is no last enemy, except death and even that's been conquered. Every victory brings a new enemy. I have noticed that after a pastor takes a church and goes through a building program, he or she generally goes through a great personal crisis of some kind. After a woman has a baby she often has postpartum depression. After you go through the building phase you must be prepared for the new phase of the journey. It is in that phase that many fail.

4. The Necessity of a Covering

What happens when there are no more arks to build? What do you do when the urgency produced by adversity has passed? Noah returned to his *normal* life as a farmer. What happened next? He got drunk. He was now drinking from his own labor and works. He had lost sight of God. His focus was now on himself.

Let me just say that *your resource is not your source.* When you start looking to your personal resources to complete the task, you are in trouble. The thing that keeps me going is that I know I cannot count on myself. I must always make God my source. If I were trusting in myself I would be finished by now. I turn to God in the urgency of the moment.

Noah lost his urgency. He lost his vision. How could that have happened? After all that he had just experienced, how could he have ended up in his tent, drunk and naked? How could someone who had so clearly heard God's warning, moved into action, built a boat, and survived the storm get drunk and naked on the floor of his tent? How can someone who has watched people get healed, who has seen mighty miracles, and done great things, end up in a bar drunk out of his mind? It happens. You want me to list those in recent times? I covered up a drunk evangelist at a conference who was sleeping it off under my book table. I followed another into Avis rental return at DFW to see the backseat loaded with empty beer cans. I've been around too long, folks.

In the early days of this country's history the British tried to defeat the Native Americans. But their style of war was no match for this fierce enemy. While the British marched into battle in their normal way, the Indians were jumping out of trees screaming and yelling and attacking the British. What did the British do to defeat the American Indian? They introduced them to Fire Water—alcohol. Guys will use alcohol so that they can get a girl drunk and have sex with her—so that their "no" will become a "yes."

Noah wasn't some wino begging for money on a street corner. He had just saved his family from one of the world's greatest calamities. He allowed himself to celebrate his victory with alcohol rather than worship.

It is important that every one of us has someone who watches over our life.

You can get drunk on a lot of things—not just alcohol. You know that by now, I'm sure. Some people get drunk on riches, others on power. The important thing to note is that they have left themselves exposed and uncovered.

Noah was a great man of power and faith and yet he was drunk and naked in his tent. His sons came in and had to cover their drunken father's naked body. There is a powerful truth in this picture. I believe in the power of covering. It is important that every one of us has someone who watches over our life—someone who can speak into our life. We must be accountable to someone or we will be accountable to no one. I am not talking about legalism or control or some weird shepherding thing. I am talking about powerful relationships where we have someone who cares about our life enough to protect us from our insanity.

Christianity is not a walk for the solitary and independent. In the context of community we should find a covering for ourselves—a covering that protects us from ourselves.

Bad things happen when you leave yourself uncovered. Ham came into the tent and saw his father's nakedness. He went and told Shem and Japheth and they covered him up. When Noah woke up, the Bible says that he knew something was wrong.

Noah knew that his youngest son had done something evil in that tent while he was drunk. We are not exactly sure what happened in that tent. Some say that Ham committed an act of incest with his mother. In Leviticus it is implied that the woman is the nakedness of the man. The other thought, which makes a little more sense to me, is that Ham went in and took advantage of Noah. Exposed and uncovered, Noah was abused by his own son.

But here is the truth. If you allow yourself to become uncovered and vulnerable there will be those who take advantage of you. The enemy wants you to be drunk so that he can take advantage of you. It doesn't matter if you are drunk on power or drunk on riches. Someone is going to sneak up on you and abuse you.

Drunkenness makes you think you are stronger than you are and gives you a false sense of judgment. Getting drunk on yourself and your desires will block the power of the Spirit to assist you in life. That is a very dangerous place. The church is not exempt from this kind of stupor. There are too many preachers who are drunk on their own self-importance. They spend millions of dollars on promoting themselves, rather than Christ. They do not understand that just as quickly as they went up the ladder, they can come down that fast.

When we allow ourselves to get drunk on things, we expose ourselves to all kinds of exploitation.

5. The Risk of a Curse

Noah's nakedness and Ham's abuse was a double whammy that resulted in the curse of a whole nation. As it happened with Noah and Ham so it could happen to us, and is happening in our world. Just look at the generation of children and young people who are lost. In this country that was founded on godly principles, who would have ever thought that preschoolers would be expelled from school because of anger and violence and bringing guns to the classroom? Who would have thought that stone-cold killers could walk into our schools and slaughter so many innocent kids?

There was a time if you were called to the principal's office you would be in tears, fearing for your life. Now kids are going to prison. You see their faces in the news—no emotion, no fear and no tears. There is no discipline and there is no accountability—no sense of right and wrong—none.

While the church and her preachers are drunk on their own self-importance and indulgent lifestyle, kids are killing kids. Our schools are being taken over by thugs and hooligans.

Our politicians have no answers. They are the ones that have opened up the legal doors that have created this insanity. While they seek to consolidate their power they are blind to the moral decline of this nation.

But you have been warned. If you allow this drunkenness to continue and if you allow yourself to remain uncovered this curse will continue. A whole generation will be lost, again.

Noah—like the prodigal son—finally came to himself. What is it going to take for some folks to come to themselves? Maybe in the tragedy of our times there will be those who come to themselves— those who awake from this silly stupor—and commit themselves to turn this nation back to God. Maybe it will take the agony of defeat and the testing by great storms, or another Great Depression, or another world war. Far fetched? Think again. Maybe, at that point, the prodigal will come home to the Father.

I do have hope. As I watch the young people who come to this ministry they give me hope for this nation. Maybe it is going to take a new generation that will help us find the compass we have lost and lead us out of this malaise of folly and insanity. There are a growing number in this generation who are rejecting the ways of the past. They are intent and intense about serving God. They have heard the warning and are prepared to build something new in this world. Maybe it's a throwback to the 60s where young people really do want to do something with their lives.

It is time to become what God intended us to be.

I am sensing it now. Everywhere I go I am starting to see a new passion for God. This passion will upset a few people. Those who are content with the status quo will not like this new surge of violence against the old systems of man. It will create an anxiety that strikes fear in the heart of those who are content with their own selfish ways.

This is our day. The time is now. When the alarm goes off this time, it is not the time to hit the snooze button. It is time to come to ourselves. It is time to free ourselves from generational curses. It is time to become what God intended us to be. We are warned. We are moving. We are building. We know the price tag is high. We will not be uncovered. And we will reverse the curse of the past generations!

8

THE VERSE THAT REVERSED THE CURSE

"Hope begins in the dark, the stubborn hope that if you just show up and try to do the right thing, the dawn will come. You wait and watch and work: you don't give up."[28]

THE BOOK OF GENESIS is the book of beginnings. In this ancient manuscript we find the beginning of all things—of the heavens and the earth, of light and darkness, of seas and skies, of land and vegetation, of sun and moon and stars, of sea and air and land animals, of human beings (made in God's own image, the climax of His creative activity), of marriage and family, of society and civilization, of sin and redemption, and of failure and prophetic promises. The grace of God reigns in every chapter. Man fails—God saves.

The quote, "The opera ain't over until the fat lady sings," supposedly originated with San Antonio sports broadcaster Dan Cook during a television newscast in April 1978. He coined the famous phrase after the first basketball game between the San Antonio Spurs and the Washington Bullets during the 1977-78 NBA playoffs, to illustrate that while the Spurs had won once, the series was not yet over. According to "The Washington Post," June 11, 1978, p. D6, Cook "said his line was a takeoff on Yogi Berra's line, 'The game isn't over 'til it's over,'" and this story behind the saying is recorded in the Library of Congress. Well, the fat lady never sings in this human drama because God continues to rescue man from his slippery slide.

Genesis lays the foundation for the beginning of mankind. It is a human book, a book about human relations. There is no attempt to cover up the truth in these stories. You will see man in his raw form, with all of his shamefaced deeds and his heroic actions of faith.

Genesis really is the theological foundation of everything that we hold true—the love of God, the sinful nature of man, the promise of redemption, and the covenants with the community of God. God made man and immediately gave him a home, mankind's first home. The earth was created as a special place for the manifestation of His love and the outworking of His plans. God called this home the Garden of Eden, a place uniquely formed for the son of His love. Giving special and loving regard to the formation of this perfect setting for Adam, it would be the model for all future homes—furnished with love, freedom, acceptance, creativity, companionship and peace.

There was a plan from the very beginning—a divine purpose—and God would use man as His instrument to fulfill that plan. Then something happened. In the process of fulfilling that plan man took a bad turn.

The Blame Game

Sandwiched in this human drama is a prophetic promise demonstrating God's intention to reverse the curse created by Satan. The third chapter opens with a devilish plot that will seek to destroy God's crowning act of creation—man. Spinning his treacherous web Satan fashions a subtle trap that causes a rupture in the purposes of God.

God is the king of asking the right question.

With one bite of the fruit from the tree of good and evil they fell and then they ran and hid. Running from God—this is the natural tendency of man. Look at your own life. Whenever your life is falling apart, you want to hide from God. We want to run from God. Isn't that interesting? After the fall the Bible says in Genesis 3:8 that God was walking in the cool of the garden. He sensed man's presence in the bushes and presented a question, "Adam, where are you?" (v. 9). God is the king of asking the right question.

And Adam came out from behind the bushes. He was hiding from God. God confronted him. "How did this happen? How could you let this happen?" (v. 11). And like any normal, red-blooded man, he pointed to his wife and said in verse 12, "It's her fault. It's *her* fault." As we have already stated, hiding and blaming only increase man's problems. This is the circuitous route of the blame game. 'A' feels guilty about their action. 'A' looks for a rationale to put the blame on someone else. 'A' blames 'B.'

Many marriages have been destroyed by this selfish game. When something goes wrong in the marriage we are quick to blame the other person. "You don't talk to me." "You make fun of me in public." "You never notice me." Around and around we go and the cycle never ends until we realize that we are responsible for our own actions.

When you assume no responsibility for the issues in your home, you have created a very unhealthy environment. If you really believe that the problem is totally someone else's, then you're at the mercy of that person. If they don't change, then you are locked into their issues. In order to be successful in life one must take charge of his life. He cannot be paralyzed by the opinions and actions of others. We must take responsibility for ourselves—for our own actions, attitudes and emotions. Somebody has to be spiritual enough to step up and say, "I was wrong. Let's make this thing right." Otherwise, you will continue to go around and around on the circle of the blame game. Adam blamed Eve. Eve blamed the devil (v. 13), and the circle never ends. Someone must stop the cycle.

Many of us have let a relationship deteriorate and die because we were waiting for someone else to step up and say, "I was wrong." It isn't about who is right or wrong. It's about, "Let's get the thing right. Let's get the problem solved."

The beautiful love story now turns out to be a real soap opera. The whole thing is a mess. And we're all the recipients of their dysfunction. Just like Adam and Eve, we need somebody to blame. Blame

Adam. Blame Eve. Blame the devil. We all want to blame some-body. Television and radio is full of dysfunctional people playing the blame game—Jerry Springer, Dr. Phil, Dr. Laura, and on and on. We watch the parade of people who come on these shows, and we keep trying to find functional, normal people. I wish somebody could find me one normal, functional person. Find me one. There are none. We all have our issues.

All this human dysfunction goes back to the first family. We can trace our heritage and our history and our issues all the way back to the first family who ever lived on planet earth. We've inherited this dysfunction from them. The Bible calls this dysfunction, sin. They bypassed their DNA on to us.

The Verse that Reversed the Curse

The first family was in shambles. The whole plan was falling apart. Not to worry. For every devilish action there is an equal and even more powerful divine reaction that corrects all that Satan would seek to do. The first messianic promise is right there in the third chapter and it counters Satan's ploy.

> *And I will put enmity between thee and the woman, and between thy seed and her seed; it shall bruise thy head, and thou shalt bruise his heel.*
> —Genesis 3:15

This is the first promise about the coming Messiah. From out of the woman something is going to come forth. Something is going to be pushed out of the woman. From the womb of the one who failed will come One who will be their redemption. The Messiah is going to bruise the head of the serpent. That was a prophecy, a promise. Eve didn't have the luxury of reading the whole Bible. She didn't know how the story was going to play out. She was in the story and had no clue as to how God would fulfill His promise. But I am sure of this. When she got the promise, when she heard it, she was encouraged. She got some hope with that word from God. Yes, Adam and Eve made huge mistakes. Their mistakes created a virus—a germ that still infects humanity.

They were afraid to face up to their disobedience. They blamed each other. But in the midst of the pain produced by their blunders, God gave the first couple a promise. He would deliver them from the curse! The seed of the woman would rise up and bruise the head of the serpent, and the serpent would bruise the heel. Their salvation was in her womb. God would provide a way to break the cycle of sin and destruction. He would free them from the bondage of the enemy and his evil ways.

That's a great prophecy. *"I'm gonna produce something someday that's gonna turn this thing around. I may be in a mess now. There may be a problem. I may have bought into temptation. I may have messed this whole thing up, and maybe I was the one to blame. But thank God, God has promised me that I'm gonna be a part of the solution."*

There is no god like our God. He is a redeeming God. We cannot save ourselves from our human tragedy, but He can. He is the One who has the power to reverse our curses. He can deliver us from our addictions. He can save us from our dilemmas. He can heal us from our pain. He can wipe away our sorrows.

Adam and Eve were wrestling with their guilt and shame but God gave them a promise that brought joy back to them. They now had hope for the future based upon this prophecy of the One who will come and deal a deathblow to the enemy.

What Happened to that Prophecy?

Eve held on to the promise and waited with expectation for that *one*. Can you imagine the excitement and the anticipation when she knew that she was pregnant? That's good, isn't it? The prophecy was made. And now it looked like the prophecy was about to be fulfilled. Are you with me so far? Are you following the story? Now she was pregnant. Will this be the answer to the promise? I can hear her now. "I'm going to get you now, Devil. I'll bruise your head. I'm going to give birth to One who will bring you down. You're finished, Devil. You're done. I'm going to bruise your head. I will be the messenger, the conduit for the promise of God."

And the Bible says in Genesis 4:1 that Adam *knew* Eve. That is Bible talk. It means that they had sex and then Eve got pregnant. She gave birth to Cain and then had a second child that they named Abel. I am sure that Adam and Eve tried to raise their young boys with the knowledge of God and His purposes for the earth. I have a feeling that Eve told them about the promise. In fact, I have a feeling that she thought her sons were the answer to the promise. One or both of them could bring an end to this plague of sin. She had high hopes and much anticipation.

But as we've talked about, life doesn't always pan out the way you think it's going to. Have you ever thought that something was going to happen that would change your life for the better? Did you ever have great plans and were so convinced that your future was bright? You had a prophecy, a promise. There is a funny thing about prophecy. Its words are always cryptic and full of double meaning. What we think it means just might not be what we thought.

There are times when a prophetic word will give direction, but most of us should be able to figure out what the Word of God says for us.

There is another troubling thing about prophecy. There are too many people out there who don't have a clue what they are doing and are giving words to people. They raise people's hopes about things they have never seen. The last thing about prophecy that bothers me is this need in the Charismatic/Pentecostal community to "get a word from God." Everyone is running around trying to get a word. Don't get me wrong, there are times when a prophetic word will give direction, but most of us should be able to figure out what the Word of God says for us.

Why are you always going to man to get a word? Why can't you get it from God? Have you ever heard of prayer? Have you ever heard that God can speak to you through His Word? God gave you a brain. He thought enough about the importance of the brain that He protected it with a skull. Now He expects you to read His book, use that brain and walk in obedience. *This is the way, walk ye in it* (Isaiah 30:21).

You need to know the Bible for yourself. Don't worry about somebody else trying to give you the interpretation. Know it for yourself. Don't do what you've been taught, do what it says. What did Paul tell his student, Timothy? *Study to shew thyself approved unto God, a workman that needeth not to be ashamed, rightly dividing the word of truth* (2 Timothy 2:15).

Eve had high hopes. But as we are going to see, her hopes came crashing down. Sometimes things don't work out and you find yourself in a place questioning what happened to your high hopes.

What in the world happened in my life? My life was going smooth. I was doing so well. My life was successful. My marriage was going great. I was growing. I felt good. I was studying. I felt like God was blessing me. And then all of a sudden, boom! Life blows up in your face. Have you been there? If not, you will be.

Eve expected a promise to be fulfilled, a prophecy to be manifested. But, in the middle of her high expectation, a fight broke out. Cain grew up and became a farmer and Abel became a sheepherder. Something happened one day, and Cain started a fight with his brother. I work with guys who are pretty good fighters. They have grown up in the streets and are very tough guys. They carry knives and guns. They know Tae Kwon Do, Jiu Jitsu, and all those other kinds of martial arts. They have never backed down from a fight. I tell these kids that I am not impressed with how well they can fight. They don't impress me. Do you know why? They haven't seen a fight until they have seen a church fight.

There is nothing meaner than a church fight. I've seen fist fights right in the middle of a board meeting in a church. There's no telling what you'll see when the "Board of Demons" gets together. It's crazy. I can't believe how crazy people can get in church when they don't get their way. I've never seen so much anger over such petty things.

Cain and Abel had a fight and religion has been fighting ever since—Christians killing Jews, Catholics and Protestants fighting each other, Moslems killing Christians. It's crazy. All the fighting we're seeing around the world in Israel, Palestine, Lebanon, Iraq, and Belfast. It's all over religion. Religious people can be the meanest people. The history of the church is filled with blood—inquisitions, crusades, and wars. It is all in the name of religion.

It hasn't stopped. We might not kill each other today, but we do kill each other with our words. Church people argue over the craziest things. Some like it quiet in worship and others like it loud and demonstrative and a fight breaks out. Is that crazy or what?

The first fight in the human drama was about worship. Interesting, isn't it? Genesis 4:4 says that God received Abel's sacrifice, but not Cain's. Cain got jealous because his brother had more favor, and God had accepted his worship. You haven't been in a fight unless you're in a fight with somebody who is jealous of you.

You are probably familiar with the story. Cain got angry and his jealousy became a seed of destruction. Cain tricked Abel into meeting him in the field. Abel was the innocent one and thought no ill of his brother, and so he went out to meet Cain in the field. Verse 8 tells us that while talking in the field, Cain rose up and killed his only brother. There goes the prophecy!

Cain attempted to cover up his sin (v. 9). And here came God. The Bible says God came walking through the field and asked Cain a question, "Where is your brother?" Again, God had a question for man. God used the power of a question to expose Cain to his sin.

How did Cain get out of this? He responded with his own question. "Am I my brother's keeper?" Cain had learned well. He used the power of the cover-up to avoid the real issue. Actually, the answer to his question is, "Yes." Yes, you are your brother's keeper. At this point the story began to unravel. We now have a dead boy killed by the older brother. Can you picture the human side of this tragedy? Eve believed her boys were part of the promise. She thought one of these boys was going to be the fulfillment of the prophecy.

And in the process of that fight, she actually lost both sons. She lost them both. She lost one to death, and the other one to a curse. God cursed Cain to wander as a vagabond for the remainder of his life. Rather than reversing the curse, it appeared as though the curse would continue.

There is no pain like the pain in your own house, because you can never get away from it.

The Pain of Promise Lost

There is no pain like the pain in your own house. Why? Because you can never escape this pain. It is always there. There is no pain like the pain in your own house, because you can never get away from it. It follows you every day. When you wake up, when you go to bed, you live with the tension and sorrow caused by the torture in your own house. You live with the angst and damage caused by the betrayal of love. The home should be a place of love and safety. You should feel secure in your own home.

When you are sexually or physically abused, the shock of betrayal can be overwhelming. When one of your partners physically abuses you or commits adultery, the pain seems more than you can handle. The home has become a house of horror. You can't go to sleep at night because of fear that someone will come into your room and touch you.

This kind of pain struck Adam's household. They were horrified when they got the news of their son's death. It was a double whammy. Their one son was dead and the other was a murderer and cursed. In one day they had lost both sons! What is a mother to do? Mothers seem to feel this pain greater than dads. They take it into their heart and suffer greatly. Eve was the first mom to suffer the pain of losing a son. All of her hopes, her dreams, and her goals for her precious boys are now gone. She is left with only a mountain of questions. What happened to the promise? What happened to the prophecy? Now who's going to bruise the head of the serpent? Who will save us?

In her torment, her questions turn to blame. "But God, You said! You promised! Where is Your word? What is going to happen? Where is Your power? How could You let this happen?"

But God

But God. This phrase can be seen as an accusation or an alteration. "But God" can express our anger at the disappointment that God did not keep His word. "But God" can also mean except for God. With these words we are either accusing God or we are understanding that He is altering our situation. Except for God, we would be lost and hopeless. "But God" either brings anger or it releases hope.

Paul understood this concept. He understood the hopeless condition of the human soul. In writing to the church at Ephesus, Paul wrote: *But God, who is rich in mercy, for his great love wherewith he loved us, Even when we were dead in sins, hath quickened us together with Christ, (by grace ye are saved)* (Ephesians 2:4-5). When things start spiraling out of control let me remind you, it ain't over till it's over.

As long as you are breathing, there is hope for your life!

Eve thought it was over. There would be no promise because there was no son. It looked like the promise would never be fulfilled. Have you ever felt like a failure? Have you ever felt like your life was finished? Have you ever felt like you had your shot at it and you missed it, and now you're condemned to walk around like a fool with **FAILURE** tattooed on your forehead?

This is a lesson you HAD better learn: it ain't over 'till it's over. When it looks like all your dreams have become nightmares, when it looks like all your expectations have become disasters, this is not the time to give up. I don't care how bad it looks. I don't care what your past is. I don't care how bad a situation you've come out of. There is always hope. As long as you are breathing, there is hope for your life!

Can you imagine what Eve was feeling? One of her sons had been murdered. I cannot think of a greater pain, except that the murderer is your other son. The agony she must have suffered was beyond human description. These were her boys and she loved them greatly. She'd had such great expectations for them and now…they were both gone.

The conflict of feelings must have been terrible. Cain was her beloved eldest son. But Cain killed her baby boy. What do you do with the person you love who killed the other person you love? She felt sorrow for Cain and this whole mess he had gotten himself into. On the other hand, she was angry with him. With a tinge of guilt she actually felt hatred for her only son. You think you've got problems. You don't have problems like Eve had. Put yourself right in this story. What would you do?

Another Promise—The Curse is Again Reversed

Never count God out. As long as there is God, there is hope. God always has an answer, even for the most tragic human situation.

And Adam knew his wife again; and she bare a son, and called his name Seth: For God, said she, hath appointed me another seed instead of Abel, whom Cain slew.
                                                        —GENESIS 4:25

She called his name Seth. This is the verse that reversed the curse. The curse of man is reversed by the promise of God.

Eve was torn apart with pain. She was emotionally distraught. This was not a time to be thinking about sex. She wanted nothing to do with Adam. She was wallowing in her sorrow. Can you imagine Adam leaning over to Eve, "Come on, baby." She instantly responded, "Not tonight." The last time they conceived it brought her great regret. She would not go through this again. The bedroom was the beginning of the painful process of what she had just gone through. You think she wanted to go through that again? I don't think so.

So Adam put on his best cologne. He made himself as appealing as possible and approached his wife, lying on the bed weeping for her sons. Adam must be crazy, but he approached his wife. I think she must have looked at him and said, "I have a headache." There it was. Spoken like a true woman.

Why would Eve even consider starting all over again? She was no masochist. She was not going to afflict herself again. Looking at Adam she questioned him, "Why would you want to do that? That's why I'm in pain. You're talking about intimacy, and I'm still in pain. Leave me alone. Don't touch me. Don't touch me." See one of the hardest things to do is to break through somebody's pain with intimacy. When someone you love has hurt you, you begin to build walls around yourself. It is a protective mechanism that kicks in gear to shield us from future heartache. You refuse to allow anyone into your life. You associate intimacy with hurt so you avoid intimacy. It's like trying to pick up your dog after it's been hit by a car. It will try to bite you even though you're trying to help. The pain is too much.

That's why it's difficult for young women who have been abused emotionally, mentally, or physically to open up when they get married. This is why pastoral counseling is so important. You must find a way to short circuit the defense mechanism and tear down the walls you have built or you will never be able to enjoy the power of love again. Even if you are a Christian and think your issues have been resolved, you can still be wrestling with intimacy issues. Sometimes, they are buried so deep that others don't see them and then when you get married they flare up. You must find a place of healing for your pain.

"Not tonight, Adam. I can't do this again," Eve said. "I am not going to do it again. I'm worn out. God said He was going to save us. God has failed me. You think I want to set myself up to walk through this hell again? Are you crazy? Leave me alone."

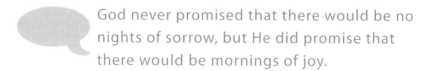

God never promised that there would be no nights of sorrow, but He did promise that there would be mornings of joy.

Somehow, Adam leaped over her walls and through the wooing of a loving husband, Genesis 4:25 says, *And Adam knew his wife again*.... Again. In that verse, I look at it as though the Holy Spirit is bragging, "You are agonizing over your condition. You have given up all hope. You have built your walls to protect yourself," but the Holy Spirit comes along and says, "Yes, we're going to do this again. We're going to do this one more time." God broke through and His word came to her again.

Hope was resurrected. Somewhere along the way a new promise came to her. Eve said, "For God has appointed me another seed instead of Abel, whom Cain slew." She now understood that the curse had again been reversed. God had turned Eve's mourning into laughter. She now has the son of promise. ... *Weeping may endure for a night, but joy cometh in the morning* (Psalm 30:5). God never promised that there would be no nights of sorrow, but He did promise that there would be mornings of joy. Eve found her joy in Seth, the son of promise.

Adam had to break through the walls and the struggle and the pain of his wife. In the same way the Holy Spirit is trying to break through the distress that is in your life. He's trying to break down the walls you have built to keep everyone out. He's trying to break down the defenses produced to protect you from the pain in this world. I know that you trusted God and still got hurt. I know that you have trust issues. I know that others have created disillusionment in your life. I am here telling you that you must once again trust Him. You must open up your life to Him again. This is your only hope. There's a promise at stake. There is a promise that is still waiting for you.

Take a Chance

God has appointed something else for you. This is not the end of your life. It is the beginning of something new and wonderful. It is the power of an appointment. If you make a doctor's appointment three weeks from now, you mark it on your calendar and you start counting it down. Two weeks later you still have an appointment, don't you? A week later, you still have an appointment. You don't have an appointment the day you have an appointment. You had that appointment three weeks before you ever had the appointment.

Do you understand what I'm telling you? In the midst of your struggles, God has already appointed something else for your life. Yes, a lot of stuff has happened in the period of time before the appointment. But you still have an appointment. Something is still going to happen. God has an appointment for you. It is marked on the calendar of your life, and if you will not give up, the appointment will happen. He has promised, and He will keep His appointment with you.

Have you ever felt like something in your life was pulling you, but you couldn't explain it? Did you ever feel like you were *supposed* to say something or do something or go somewhere and you can't really understand it? Have you ever had that feeling? It's like, "I have to do this. It's an appointment. I have no choice." That is God drawing you.

> *For the vision is yet for an appointed time, but at the end it shall speak, and not lie: though it tarry, wait for it; because it will surely come, it will not tarry.*
> —Habakkuk 2:3

Cain, Abel, Seth. Cain, Abel, Seth. Cain, Abel, Seth. Eve thought it was all falling apart, didn't she? She thought there was no way in the world that her promise would ever come to pass. She thought her life was over. How could she be sure it would turn out differently this time? She had trusted before and where did it get her? But Eve took a risk. She conceived and had another son.

You have to be willing to risk all if you are going to see your promise. Your future is wrapped up in your willingness to take a risk. Yes, people have hurt you. Yes, you have experienced disillusionment and disappointment. But, you must risk again. Your future and the future of others depend on it.

God made a promise. Whatever God promises, He will fulfill. It may not be fulfilled the way you think it is going to be fulfilled. It may not come at the time when you think it is supposed to come. But if you stay faithful, God will turn your pain into a promise. It is a process but through the process you will find the promise. It will be a new beginning.

> *This month shall be unto you the beginning of months: it shall be the first month of the year to you.*
> —Exodus 12:2

God knows how to wipe out the past and create new beginnings. He can take *this* month and make it like the first month of the rest of your life. He can take your October and make it into your January, the first day of the rest of your life. It doesn't matter how young or how old you are. God has a new beginning for you. He can erase the chalkboard of your life and make it clean. The negative words that people have written over your life can be removed in one clean swipe of His powerful hand.

Cain, Abel, Seth. Chapter four of Genesis is about murder and grief and lost dreams. But it is also about rebirth and joy and dreams that came true. It is about people who endured their pain and were willing to take another risk. Their risk was rewarded with a promise that was fulfilled.

Rewriting Your History

> *This is the book of the generations of Adam. In the day that God created man, in the likeness of God made he him; Male*

and female created he them; and blessed them, and called their name Adam, in the day when they were created. And Adam lived an hundred and thirty years, and begat a son in his own likeness, and after his image; and called his name Seth: And the days of Adam after he had begotten Seth were eight hundred years: and he begat sons and daughters: And all the days that Adam lived were nine hundred and thirty years: and he died.

—GENESIS 5:1-5

This is the book of generations—this is the book of stories, human stories. This is the book of how God rewrites our story. Chapter five was a totally separate scroll. It is a genealogy, a family tree. It is tracking the story of early man. There might be a better word. It's a tracking—it's a history—starting right from the very beginning. It retraces the creation of man. God created man in His image. He blessed him and called him Adam. Adam lived one hundred thirty years and then begat a son in his image. He called his son Seth. What happened to Cain and Abel? They didn't make the genealogy book. It was like they were never there. We know they were there. We have history to prove it. *But why aren't they in the book?*

Have you ever gone through something and you knew you went through it, because you lived it? You have memory of the experience and the anguish it caused. You lived through the agony. You endured the hell of that experience. You remember all of that. But God said, "It's not gonna make it to the Book. It's done. It's under the blood. It's forgiven. It is as though it never happened."

Of all the things that you've done wrong, you can do one thing right, and it will change your whole life.

Seth was the one. Seth was the one who Eve was waiting for all the time. She just didn't know it. She thought it was Cain or Abel, but it wasn't. It's like they never existed. When God takes over your life, it's not a continuation of your old life. It's a brand new one. It is a brand new life. God wants to do a brand new thing for you. What He is going to do will erase the pain of the past. The Book says when Adam had Seth he was 130 years old. He lived 800 more years. It says he had more sons and daughters. So obviously, having Seth did what? Reversed the curse. His life opened up something for an entire generation to come after them.

Of all the things that you've done wrong, you can do one thing right, and it will change your whole life. Do you understand what I'm saying? Cain, Abel, Seth! Maybe you have made a lot of mistakes. I encourage you to turn it around. Take a risk. Open up your heart to the possibilities that are around you. Let go of your pain. Embrace the promise God has for you. You did make a mess of your life. You made some serious blunders along the way. But this is a new day. God is prepared to rewrite your history with one right action on your part. God is ready to reverse the curse on your life, but it's on you now. Make the call!

9

THE SLAVE WHO BECAME A BISHOP— ONESIMUS AND PHILEMON

The illiterate of the 21st century will not be those who cannot read and write, but those who cannot learn, unlearn, and relearn.[29]

ONESIMUS WAS A RUNAWAY slave who eventually ended up in prison. He was a nobody, and if God had not intervened, his life would have disappeared in the annals of history. Being alone in prison was definitely not the end of this man's story. Onesimus actually went from total obscurity to notoriety thanks to the apostle Paul's interest in him—from being a prisoner to becoming a preacher. He transitioned from getting into trouble and being a slave in the service of Philemon to becoming a bishop of one of the most powerful and famous churches of the New Testament. His story should be an encouragement to all those who find themselves in bad places.

This is another God story, a story of how God can take a nobody and turn him (or her) into a somebody. It is my story, and I am sure it is your story. None of us were candidates for greatness, but *for those who walk with God, greatness will find them.*

I have noticed that the older I get, the more I know. Then, the more I know, the less I understand. The older we get, and sometimes the more experience we have, the more questions we encounter. Life is a constant mystery and is not easily understood. We are all born and we all die but in between we experience the mystery. Every experience should move us into a clearer understanding, but it only raises more questions. Theologians and philosophers have pondered the question of life for centuries. Job asked the question, "Why do the righteous suffer?" Examining life around him, Solomon pessimistically said, "All is vanity."

Why are there some good young people who die a tragic death? Why is it that good people seem to have more struggles than the godless crowd? It's funny, isn't it? We don't like to contemplate the tough questions. Some things in life don't make sense so we avoid the questions that plague us. We are afraid that if we talk about it too much, our faith may waiver and cause us to wonder why we are serving God. We love God. We are committed to serving Him. We try our best to walk according to His desires and yet it seems we have as many problems and conflicts as the guy next to us who doesn't care about God. Where is the advantage of serving God if we still have to suffer?

Focus and Getting the Big Picture

With all these questions dancing around in my head I have discovered some truths that help me at those times of questioning. I understand that there is a bigger picture that most of us don't see. We can only see to the corner, but God sees around the corner. So if you can only see the one who does the seeing, you'll be okay. There are things working in the invisible world that are just not made known to us. We will only discover them by *focusing.*

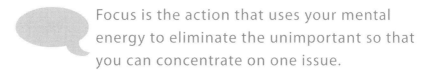

Focus is the action that uses your mental energy to eliminate the unimportant so that you can concentrate on one issue.

The best way I can explain this is going back to when I was young. All of us remember as kids how we could burn a piece of paper by taking a magnifying glass and focusing the sun's rays through the glass. If you got too far away, it would not be focused enough and if you got to close, it wouldn't work. You had to move the magnifying glass in and out until it found the right focus point and then the paper would begin to burn.

When our minds are bombarded with many thoughts, we get confused and lose the power of focus. Focus is the action that uses your mental energy to eliminate the unimportant so that you can concentrate on one issue. If you're going after something, you have to focus on that one thing. The cat that chases two mice loses both! Focus is one way of resolving problems. But like the illustration of the magnifying glass, you can get too close and miss the big picture. A part of effective focusing is being able to zoom out in your thinking and envision all of the important parts of what you are considering. There is a difference in *microscopic* thinking and *telescopic* thinking.

By microscopic thinking we can make the world smaller and see things in their individual parts. Through telescopic thinking we can see that the world is much larger and we can envision the big picture. Focus is one of the steps of effective learning.

The Power of a Letter

Life is always changing, and hopefully we are always learning. When we stop learning, we stop growing. You're either growing or dying. There is no such thing as maintaining personally. Too often, education is wasted on the young because they think they know everything. Truth will come to us when we are ready for it—when we are seeking it. That is how I approach the Bible. I never take the attitude that I know it all. I'm still a student. I am always looking to discover new truth that will help me and will help others. One of the things that I've struggled with from time to time is the story of Philemon. I was trained in hermeneutics (the principles of biblical interpretation). I know how to define the Scriptures. But sometimes the principles don't seem to work. Sometimes the truth of the test seems to elude us.

The book of Philemon doesn't seem to make sense to me. I've wondered why it is even in the Bible. The book of Psalms makes perfect sense to me. The songs of David have given us great encouragement. The book of Romans makes sense. It is the heart of the gospel of Jesus. The Gospels make perfect sense. I get it. But the book of Philemon just does not make sense. What possessed the early scholars to put this book into the canon? How did it even make it in?

Philemon wasn't an apostle. What was so special about him? He was just a cell group leader. It's not even a book, to my mind. In fact, it is not even a letter. It's a postcard. It only has one chapter. It doesn't have the depth of theology contained in the other books that Paul wrote.

But the more I think about it, right now, as I sit here, it may make some sense. There's a reason it's in there. How long has it been since you wrote a hand-written letter? With the launch of the computer age there are fewer and fewer people who know how to write a letter. Everything is e-mail—short and succinct. I am a strange creature. I don't use the computer. When I write a letter, I want somebody to know that I took the time to sit down and write to them. I still write thank-you notes. I think it's important. Computers make life faster and easier, but they have robbed us of the personal. There is nothing personal about getting an e-mail in the midst of all the other junk that is flowing into our mail box. I believe a personal, hand-written letter has much more significance.

Letters have meaning. There are love letters, thank-you letters, birthday letters—letters are birthed in relationship. Every letter has been birthed out of a relationship and created with a purpose. I don't sit down and write just to write. I have a purpose. You write something with purpose.

A Letter to Philemon

As most of you know, three very different characters are found in this letter—Paul, Philemon and Onesimus. Paul wrote the letter.

Philemon received the letter. And the letter is about Onesimus, who was Philemon's slave.

Theologians have debated as to whether or not Paul should have gotten involved in the slave issue. There are some who think Paul should have taken this opportunity to condemn Philemon and the whole issue of slavery. It is interesting that none of the New Testament writers condemned slavery.

Shouldn't Paul have taken the occasion to sound an alarm against the injustice of slavery? Maybe Paul should have taken the time to write a treatise on the problem of slavery in the Roman culture. Perhaps he should have encouraged people to boycott all goods produced by slave labor. Maybe Paul should have launched an organization, "Christians Against Slavery."

Slavery was a common practice in the time of the Romans. In fact, slavery was a common practice dating back to the Egyptians. It was a normal thing to make slaves out of vanquished people or to purchase slaves from the barbarians. The Roman economy and life were heavily dependent upon slave labor. The practice of slavery has been in force since the time of recorded history—since the time of William Wilberforce (1759-1833), the British politician, philanthropist, and the man who led the way for abolishing the British slave trade. His stand against slavery led to the passage of the Slave Trade Act of 1807 in England.

I lived during the time in American history when there were three bathrooms in public places—one for men, one for women, and one for coloreds, as persons of color were then called. You may have no idea what I'm talking about, but I lived during that time. I lived when there was a water fountain for whites and one for "coloreds." We all know the horrific history of slavery in this country. We know that it took men like Martin Luther King, Jr. to help turn the tide and make racial equality a reality in this country.

There were Roman philosophers in the times of Paul, like Seneca, who spoke out against the ill treatment of slaves, but the purpose of this letter from Paul to Philemon about Onesimus is much more personal than resolving the issue of slavery. The letter is about *friendship* and *forgiveness.* It is about recognizing the value of a human life.

The Good Thing in You

I thank my God, making mention of you always in my prayers, hearing of your love and faith which you have toward the Lord Jesus and toward all the saints, that the sharing of your faith may become effective by the acknowledgment of every good thing which is in you in Christ Jesus.

—PHILEMON 4-6 NKJV

The acknowledgment of every good thing—before Paul addressed the issue at hand, he prayed for his friend Philemon. Philemon and Paul had a history together. Paul led Philemon to Christ. Paul was responsible for the ongoing training of this disciple of the Lord. He let Philemon know that he saw good things in him. Philemon was a good man. He had a reputation as a man who had great love for the saints and great faith in God. Paul told Philemon that as he shared his faith, it would become active and energized as he acknowledged (the literal Greek is *epignosis,* meaning "to understand, to recognize, to have knowledge of") every good thing in him.

Paul connected the sharing of his faith with the acknowledgment of the good things in him. This is the power of a testimony—sharing the good things that have happened in your life. There is a power—an energy—that is released when people hear what God has done in your life. It creates *hunger* in other people's lives. This is evangelism at its very core.

If you are going to be a leader, then there are some things that you must understand.

The letter was a teaching prayer. Through his prayer, Paul was teaching Philemon about the power of sharing his experiences with others. I have a very large staff here in New York. I take that responsibility very seriously. I want each member of the staff to understand the foundations of what it means to walk with and serve God. I want them to understand the good things that God has done in them. I want them to understand that life is a process and they need to know how to survive and succeed in the process of life.

Paul was trying to communicate in his own inimitable way to his friend Philemon the truth of what it means to serve God. If you are going to understand life…if you are going to understand the Gospel…if you are going to be a leader, then there are some things that you must understand.

As I said, I am still learning. I have been in ministry for 40 years. Guess what? I am still learning. I am still studying. I am still asking questions. I am still looking for answers. I put 15-20 hours a week into studying the Scriptures. I do it for me, and in doing it for me, I do it for others. I believe that when you teach, you're taught. That's the beauty of teaching. When you teach others, it forces you to study. It is not enough to just share information. The goal of teaching is that others will learn. Henrietta Mears, the founder of Gospel Light Sunday School curriculum, once said, "The teacher has not taught until the pupil has learned."

It's not enough to get up and exercise your mouth about nonsensical stuff. Teaching is not getting up and putting on a show. Acting is for the movies. You have not taught until the pupil has learned, until those who are listening have comprehended and connected with the truth. There's a difference between comprehension and connection. You can understand something with your head, but until it reaches your heart and is manifested in your life, you have not learned.

You have to understand all the things that Christ has done in you, that He has done for you, and that He is doing through you. This happens when you begin to share your faith. When you do this, you begin to understand the truth. Real truth is not static. Truth must be functional and practical. Truth becomes active when we share it with others.

Sharing the Truth

The reason why the American church and most every other church I know, all over this world are by and large ineffective, is because they are not evangelistic. They are more concerned about their programs than the world around them that does not know God.

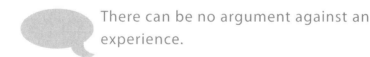

There can be no argument against an experience.

I guarantee that when you get to the place where you are quick to share your faith about the good things that Christ has done in you, that sharing releases something within you. It releases the power of the Holy Ghost, and it opens doors that could never be otherwise opened. There can be no argument against an experience.

The person with an experience is stronger than the person with an argument.

In London's Hyde Park, there is an open forum where people can get up and talk about whatever they want. They will yell and shout out their arguments. You see almost the same thing in the English Parliament. You will see them yelling and trying to shout each other down. People will argue about social issues, doctrine, and politics. People will want to challenge what you believe. They might be able to challenge you on a lot of things, but they will not be able to argue with you on your own experience and how God has changed your life.

When you begin to *share* your faith, what Christ has done in you, for you, and through you, it opens up a level of understanding of how life can work for the listener. The Greek word for sharing is *koinonia.* It indicates that in the sharing there is a fellowship, a union that happens when people get together and share their experiences. When you share your spiritual experiences, you draw people into the center of your world where God is at work.

Here's the risk. When you open up your heart to share with others you take a chance on getting burned. When you begin to love others, opening your heart to them, and inviting them into your life without reservation, that is risky business. I have openly shared my heart with thousands of people over the years, but when people betray your trust, it is hard to go back down that road again.

But there is another risk that is greater and that is letting your heart get hardened by the negative reactions and betrayal of others. I have watched too many older people allow their heart to harden— people who have been burned in life, and burned in relationships. You cannot do this. No matter what others do, you cannot allow your heart to harden.

It's risky. But the risk is worth the reward. What reward? It is the reward that comes when people do hear you and when they respond to your love and the sharing of your experiences. There is a huge personal reward that comes to you when you see people are changed by the power that has changed your life.

Paul told Philemon that whatever he believed—whatever God had done in his life, whatever God was doing through him, (and this applies to you also) whatever He's doing with you, and whatever He has done for you, you must let it show in your life. You must tell others. You cannot privatize your own experiences. You must let the love that God has demonstrated in your life be revealed to others. You must let love become the controlling power in your life.

Seized by Love

For the love of Christ constraineth us; because we thus judge,
that if one died for all, then were all dead.
—2 Corinthians 5:14

Paul wrote these words to the church in Corinth. This is his second letter to them. In his first letter he was trying to settle a church fight. The church had been squabbling right from its very beginning. They were fighting over the use of the gifts in the church, arguing over who sat where and how to handle divorce. Some of the folks were taking their fellow believers to court. It was out of control, so Paul wrote a corrective letter to them.

In his second letter, Paul gave them spiritual encouragement. In verse 14 of chapter five Paul was endeavoring to help them see what force motivated his life. He was not motivated by success, popularity, or power. He was motivated by the love of Christ. The Greek word there is *sunecho* and means to be held together, to be held fast and to be seized. Paul was seized and held captive by the love of Christ.

We *talk* about love, we *preach* about love, we do everything *but* love one another.

The love of Christ constrains me, it moves me, it pushes me, drives me toward some things, and it fences me in from other things. In the message of Jesus, he makes it very clear that the nature of God is love. Love is God's true essence. When we are reborn, we are reborn with that nature. Love is written into our DNA and should be reflected in all that we do. Unfortunately, some believers are born with a deformity and that love does not manifest itself in their lives. The world does not see the manifestation of that love. They see legalism, fighting, condemnation, unforgiveness and arrogance. The church has forgotten that the greatest tool of evangelism is the love of God.

We *talk* about love, we *preach* about love, we do everything *but* love one another. We can't even love ourselves, much less those around us. If you can't love yourself, how are you going to love others? If you can't forgive yourself, how can you forgive others? This is at the heart of the message in the book of Philemon—love and forgiveness.

I know that many Christians are sick of asking for forgiveness. Perhaps you are in that group. You have messed up so many times, you wonder how you can go back and ask God for forgiveness one more time. You may be thinking that if you were God, you would have given up on you a long time ago. Here's the truth of the matter. God's grace is greater than anything we can do. His love continues to reach out to us. We do not deserve it. That's what makes His love a scandal to religious folk who think they deserve God's love. His love reaches to the least of us, the ones who many of us would not waste our time on.

As it was for Paul, so it should be for us. This dynamic love of God should be the compelling force in our lives. It should stimulate us to reach out to others as God has reached out to us. This is good news and needs to be shared with the world. I find it sad the indiscriminate value we put on human life. All of life, no matter its human condition, has value in the sight of God and should have value in our eyes.

We should never let fear or people intimidate us. Why should we be afraid to publicly declare our love for Christ? Why should we allow people to terrorize us and hold us hostage to their opinions? This love of God is so wonderful, so liberating, so comforting that we should have the upper hand in every conversation. What we have is greater than anything someone else can offer.

The world is controlled by guilt and shame and existential angst and they are desperate to experience the love that we have discovered. All of us have stories to share that illustrate the power of God's love. Those stories need to be broadcast to our families, to our friends, to our coworkers, and to the world around us.

A Prisoner of Love

Paul's little postcard to Philemon is a story of love written by a prisoner of love. His love for Christ had taken him as a prisoner to Rome. Paul was quite familiar with jail. His love for Christ had already placed him in prison several times. In the fall of 60 A.D. Paul was placed on a Roman ship to be taken to Rome as a prisoner under the control of Julius, a Roman centurion. Upon his arrival in Rome, Paul was put under house arrest by the captain of the Roman guard.

While in Rome, Paul met a fugitive named Onesimus, the slave of Philemon. Onesimus was in Rome as a fugitive from the law. Onesimus had plotted his escape and when the time was right, he stole money from his master Philemon and skipped town. He left the city of Colossae and headed for Rome. Why Rome? Rome was a great hiding place for criminals and runaway slaves.

The city of Rome was a city of slaves. Some say that there were over a million slaves in Rome, about 25 percent of the total population. Rome was built and maintained by slavery. Some of the rich folk had as many as 500 slaves, and the emperor is said to have had as many as 20,000 slaves at his disposal.

If a runaway slave was caught, one of two things happened. If they returned and were contrite, the owner would simply take a branding iron and brand an "F" right on their forehead. "F" stood for fugitive. They were branded for life. If they rebelled and were not contrite, they would be crucified. Death or branding was the only fate for the runaway slave. Keeping the slaves in order had economical implications. They had to put pressure on the slaves to do their duty and not rebel. Therefore, they created severe consequences for the slave who ran away.

Onesimus was hiding in the city of Rome. He knew the consequences if he got caught. Rome was a big city and pretty easy to get lost in. He would never be caught if he just lost himself in the crowded city, but the inevitable happened. He was caught— captured by the love of God.

Somehow, Onesimus wound up with Paul. We are not exactly sure how. Maybe he was hiding in one of the catacombs and was discovered by a believer and taken to Paul. Maybe he was caught and thrown into prison and met Paul as a prisoner. One way or the other, Onesimus was now in the presence of Paul, the apostle. What a break! Of all the people he could end up with in Rome, he ended up with Paul. What are the chances of that happening in the biggest city in the world? Divine intervention is simply marvelous.

The story gets better. Paul shared with him the story of Christ and how Christ had changed his life. Under the tutelage of Paul, Onesimus became a Christian. He came clean and told Paul his whole story, how he was a slave of Philemon, stole from him, and fled to Rome.

Paul could hardly believe it. He knew this fellow Philemon. He had led Philemon to the Lord and was one of his best friends. What a coincidence! How lucky could this guy get? As a runaway slave, he had the opportunity to meet the greatest apostle of all time, and he came to Christ. The guy that led him to Christ was the best friend of his former master. Now this apostle was going to help him with his problems. Onesimus was prepared to do whatever he could to make his life right. He became a servant of Paul, helping him in whatever way he could. Seeing the change in the life of Onesimus and the service he so willingly and lovingly provided for him, Paul decided to write this little postcard to his friend Philemon.

Paul told Onesimus of his idea. "We need to let Philemon know that you're a Christian. He'll be thrilled. He'll be thrilled that you're safe. As a matter of fact, I'm going to write him a letter right now. And I've got a better idea, I'm going to let you hand deliver it." This was a great idea up until the point where he would deliver the letter. Was Paul crazy? Didn't he understand what could happen to Onesimus? But Onesimus had come to the place where he had perfect trust in his new friend and told Paul to write the letter.

We have already looked at the salutation of the letter. Now we get to the meat of the letter, the reason for Paul's postcard to Philemon.

> *For we have great joy and consolation in thy love, because the bowels of the saints are refreshed by thee, brother. Wherefore, though I might be much bold in Christ to enjoin thee that which is convenient, Yet for love's sake I rather beseech thee, being such as one as Paul the aged, and now also a prisoner of Jesus Christ.*
>
> —Philemon 7-9

This is not Paul's typical letter—no heavy doctrine, no deep revelation. It is a love note. Notice how Paul set up Philemon by bragging on him. "You are such an awesome guy. Just the thought of you warms my heart. You have such a good reputation." Basically, that was what Paul was saying to his old friend.

Then he prepared him for his request. Paul told Philemon that he (Paul) had the authority to command him (Philemon) to do whatever he wished. He was the one who was responsible for Philemon finding God. Philemon owed Paul a lot. But he took a slightly different tack. He would rather simply appeal to Philemon's good nature that God had worked in him. And so he continued.

> *I beseech thee for my son Onesimus, whom I have begotten in my bonds: Which in time past was to thee unprofitable, but now profitable to thee and to me: Whom I have sent again: thou therefore receive him, that is, mine own bowels: Whom I would have retained with me, that in thy stead he might have ministered unto me in the bonds of the gospel: But without thy mind would I do nothing; that thy benefit should not be as it were of*

*necessity, but willingly. For perhaps he therefore departed for
a season, that thou shouldest receive him for ever; Not now as
a servant, but above a servant, a brother beloved, specially to
me, but how much more unto thee, both in the flesh, and in
the Lord? If thou count me therefore a partner, receive him as
myself. If he has wronged thee, or oweth thee ought, put that on
mine account; I Paul have written it with mine own hand, I will
repay it: albeit I do not say to thee how thou owest unto me even
thine own self besides.*

—PHILEMON 10-19

I love Paul. He really knows how to write a good letter. He made
his case before Philemon, telling him that, while a prisoner, he had
met Philemon's runaway slave and led him to Christ. In essence,
he said, "I know he turned out to be a scoundrel to you, but he has
been a miracle to me. He has helped me so much in my work here
in Rome. Even though he has been so profitable to me, I want to
send him back to you, and I want you to accept him. I don't want
to command you to do this. Even though I could, I really want you
to do this from your heart. Whatever he has stolen from you, I will
repay. If you really love me (that is quite shrewd of Paul), then you
will accept him. I know that you lost him. I know that he stole from
you. But maybe there is a divine plan in this. Maybe you lost him
for a little while so that you could have him forever. He will be more
than a slave to you. He will be a brother. His value to you is so much
more now." And then Paul added his final words.

*Yea, brother, let me have joy of thee in the Lord: refresh my
bowels in the Lord. Having confidence in thy obedience, I wrote
unto thee, knowing that thou wilt also do more than I say. But
withal prepare me also a lodging: for I trust that through your*

prayers I shall be given unto you. There salute thee Epaphras, my fellowprisoner in Christ Jesus; Marcus, Aristarchus, Demas, Lucas, my fellowlabourers. The grace of our Lord Jesus Christ be with your spirit. Amen.

—PHILEMON 20-25

And Now You Know the Rest of the Story

In this little postcard we don't get the final result. We are given no clue in the writings of Paul how this thing turned out. Did Philemon receive Onesimus back? For the answer to that question, we have to go to church history. This is why I love history.

Here is the rest of the story. Paul asked Philemon if he would send Onesimus back. Onesimus had become so valuable to Paul in his work in Rome. From church history we see that Philemon did send Onesimus back to Paul. Onesimus delivered the letter to Philemon, and Philemon welcomed him, forgave him, and sent him back to Paul as Paul requested so that Onesimus could be a helper and partner in ministry.

He was now with Paul, and Onesimus watched Paul as he began to write some of his classic letters to the churches. Paul was getting old now, and he was moving toward the end of his life. Onesimus became his delivery boy. In the letter to the Colossian church we read:

*All my state shall Tychicus declare unto you, who is a beloved brother, and a faithful minister and fellowservant in the Lord: Whom I have sent unto you for the same purpose, that he might know your estate, and comfort your hearts; With Onesimus, **a faithful and beloved brother,** who is one of you. They shall make known unto you all things which are done here.*

—COLOSSIANS 4:7-9 (EMPHASIS ADDED)

"A faithful and beloved brother," Onesimus was now counted among Paul's team of servants. Aristarchus, Tychicus, Luke, Timothy—Onesimus had probably become friends with Paul's whole apostolic team. He was still a slave—a love slave of Christ and of Paul. Now he was a postman, delivering letters to the churches.

According to some theologians, Onesimus was also part of the team that delivered the letter to the church at Ephesus. Onesimus received the parchment from Paul and traveled to Ephesus to deliver the letter to them. There are those who say that Onesimus remained at Ephesus and eventually became the bishop of that city, known as a large, important city of that time and a natural center for the Christian churches.

How do we know this? Probably about 45-50 years after Onesimus landed in Ephesus, we are introduced to him again in the writings of Ignatius, one of the early church fathers of the second century. Ignatius was the Bishop of Antioch and he was being led from Antioch to Rome where he would embrace his martyrdom for Christ. On this journey he wrote a batch of seven letters to various churches throughout Asia Minor (Asia Minor corresponds to modern day Turkey). These are the last words of Ignatius before his death and he wanted to prepare the church for the future. While at Smyrna, Ignatius stopped to write a letter to the church at Ephesus. In chapter one of his letter, he wrote:

> *I have received your whole multitude in the person of Onesimus, whose love passeth utterance and who is moreover your bishop (in the flesh)—and I pray that you may love him according to Jesus Christ and that ye all may like him; for blessed is He that has granted you according to your deserving to have such a bishop.*[30]

The slave who became a bishop—now you know the rest of the story! Onesimus was a nobody, just a runaway slave, and at the end of his life we see that he has become a bishop of one of the most recognized churches in biblical times. What was possible for Onesimus is also possible for you!

 Onesimus knew how important this letter would be to future believers.

Onesimus was much older now and he was the bishop. He was the guardian of the works of Paul. Onesimus loved him and he appreciated him. He served him, but he didn't quite understand him in those early days. But he was older now, he understood what the old man was trying to accomplish, and he wanted to save those letters.

It is very possible that he had copies of all of Paul's letters. Can you see him reading those letters—reading the letter to the church at Galatians, where Paul discussed the law and grace and the fruit of the Spirit? Onesimus knew how important this letter would be to future believers. It must be saved. Then he picked up the letter to the church in Rome. Wow! This was good stuff. It was the very heart of the Gospel. Future generations would need these words. With tears in his eyes he read the letters to the churches in Colossae and Ephesus, the ones he had delivered to them. This was rich with apostolic truth. He was collecting all of these letters.

There was one more letter buried at the bottom of the pile. He had almost missed it. It really was only a postcard from Paul. It was the postcard sent to his former master, Philemon. The old bishop, the old man who was a slave, read that letter with tears running down his cheeks. He decided to take that letter so that everybody would know the story of the slave that became a bishop. They must know the power of love and the transforming grace of God. They must know what God had done in his life.

And that, my friend, is why Philemon is in the Bible. It is a story that all must read. It was his story. It was a "rags to riches" story of God's redeeming love.

If the Bible were still being written, we would all have great stories to tell there.

This letter is quite clear in its message. Paul wanted people to understand how important it is to share their story, the story of what God has done in their lives. You don't have to memorize anything to tell that story. It is indelibly written across your heart. You don't have to freak out when somebody asks you to tell your story. The story is rich in love and forgiveness, making you to leap for the opportunity to tell that story. It is a God story. It is a story of how His grace can change any life. It is a story of one-eyed kings—a story of ordinary people who do extraordinary things.

If the Bible were still being written, we would all have great stories to tell there. I know I would tell my story. I would tell about the man who stopped and picked me up. That was just a natural for him, wasn't it? His own child was dying but it was as natural as breathing for him to stop his truck, walk across the street, come up to me where I had been sitting on the curb for three days, and ask me one simple question: "Are you okay?" That was the question that put this whole concept of Metro Ministries—now the world's largest Sunday school—into motion.

He didn't have to go to a seminar to know what to do about me. He didn't have to go to four years of Bible school to figure out what needed to be done. He was simply one man who saw a need and the need became the call when he learned what had happened to me. I hadn't eaten for three days. He went and got his wife and they brought me some food and some water. It was natural, wasn't it?

He got on the phone, made a few calls, and five hours later I found myself in a church van on my way to a Christian youth camp. And for the first time in my life, I actually heard the words, "I love you." How did it all start? One man—not a pastor, not an evangelist, not a gospel singer—just a Christian who saw the poor little boy that nobody wanted. It's quite a story, isn't it? But there's so much more to it.

As I've watched the years go by, I've always wished that somehow I could tell folks more and more about all the things that have happened to me and comprised this journey that I've been on. I sometimes try to explain to the staff in New York in little segments in our Friday staff meetings called "Fireside Chats." I try to tell them how the 40 years of ministry that followed that afternoon on a Florida street corner have been a collection of incidences and experiences, both good and bad. From walking away from three airplane crashes to having my jaw broken, ribs broken, nose broken twice, three concussions, from being thrown from a building to having hepatitis, tuberculosis, and watching worms crawl out of my body alive that I'd picked up in the jungle, it's quite a story.

From speaking at some of the largest churches in the world to ministering in some of the smallest...from getting into fights with drug dealers to fighting with preachers (and not being sure which was worse), there's a lot I'd like to put in the Bible that would encourage some young men and young women—maybe even some older folks. My story might let them know for the first time or as a reminder that it's still all about ordinary people doing extraordinary things. My experience—and maybe yours—is something they make into movies. You know what I'm saying. There are still people out there who turn terrible tragedies and pain into amazingly productive lives that benefit many others. How is it that the little boy on the street corner who nobody wanted could possibly end up becoming the pastor of the largest Sunday school in the world?

That man who picked me up understood what a lot of us don't understand. Without fear, without over-thinking it, we should be able to tell our story to anyone, at anytime and in any place. I'd like to put my story in the Bible for someone's understanding—particularly for those who think they have to hear an audible voice, that think they have to be qualified to get up and speak. Yes, I'd like to put my story in there. It would convince them that God can use anyone, including them.

Philemon had no idea about the implications of what could happen when Onesimus returned to him. He was just an ordinary slave who was not a brother. He had no clue that when he embraced this slave, gave him his freedom, shared with him the love of Christ—that he would become an apostle. The slave who might have had an "F" branded on his forehead, the slave who was a thief and a runaway, this thief would deliver to the church some of the most important letters ever written. This slave would become a bishop.

That's why I continue to travel around the world. That's why this work, Metro Ministries, is in Brooklyn. That's why I've put my life in peril. I must tell my story. God has done so much for me, and I must tell that story to somebody. I should have been dead. Years ago I had psychiatrists look at me and say, "You should be in a mental institution. You shouldn't even be able to speak publicly. You shouldn't even be able to have a normal conversation with people." I know that. That's why I still get up in the morning. That's why I still drive the bus. I have a lot to be thankful for.

 Every day your life rubs shoulders with one-eyed kings who someday will do amazing things for God.

No one should have to force you to tell your story. The grace of God should be so powerful in your life that you are *compelled* to tell your story. You shouldn't have to be motivated by guilt or fear. Like Paul, you should be *constrained* by the love of Christ. I am sure that in your life there is a "somebody that appears to be a nobody" who needs to hear your story.

Every day your life rubs shoulders with one-eyed kings who someday will do amazing things for God. All they need to do is to hear your story, and your story will open up a door for them to hear the love of Jesus. Your story is a story that people are dying to hear. They live in desperate situations. They have made a mess out of their lives. If only they could hear your story, they would find hope—hope that their story might become a God story—a story of an ordinary person who does most extraordinary things. So from one one-eyed king to another—let it begin today!

ENDNOTES

Chapter 1

1 Quote is by Max Lerner and is quoted in *How Did I Get Here?*, Barbara DeAngelis, St. Martin's Press, New York, Pg. 281 © 2005

2 Carter Heyward, Copyright © ThinkExist 1999-2006, http://thinkexist.com/quotation/faith_is_a_process_of_leaping_into_the_abyss_not/202019.html

3 Pearl Buck, http://www.wisdomquotes.com/cat_solitude.html

Chapter 2

4 J. C. Penney

5 http://www.mapping.com/words.html

6 http://www.christring.org/khandie/WhatIsGreatness.htm

7 http://www.ccel.org/ccel/drummond/greatest.txt

Chapter 3

8 Quote by H.P. Liddon, *Worth Repeating*, Bob Kelly, Kregel, Grand Rapids, Michigan, © 2003, Pg. 309

9 *Shame and Grace,* Lewis B. Smedes, Harper Collins, New York, ©1993, Merles Fossum Pg. 3

10 Leo de Hartog, *Genghis Khan, Conqueror of the World,* Barnes and Noble, 1999

11 *Wikipedia, the free encyclopedia*, Genghis Khan, http://en.wikipedia.org/wiki/Genghis_Khan

CHAPTER 4

12 Ashley Montagu, *The Cultured Man,* World Publishing Company, Cleveland, Oh. ©1963, Pg. 13

13 http://classics.mit.edu/Aristotle/poetics.1.1.html

14 Augustine, Book of Confessions, Book One

15 Thomas Szasz, *The Second Sin*, Routledge, Florence, Kentucky ©1974, Pg. 29

16 *The Challenge of Jesus,* John Shea, The Thomas More Association, ©1975, Pg. 117

17 Gospel Truth, P.O. Box 6322, Orange, CA 92863. ©2000

CHAPTER 5

18 John F. Kennedy, Harper Perennial Modern Classics, San Francisco, © 2004, Pg. 225

19 http://www.lycos.com/info/marco-polo--kublai-khan.html

CHAPTER 6

20 Quote by Johann van Goethe, *The Book of Positive Quotes,* Rubicon Press, Minneapolis, MN © 1993, Pg. 494

21 Matthew Henry, *Matthew Henry's Commentary on the Whole Bible: Complete and Unabridged in One Volume,* © 1997 by Thomas Nelson, Inc., Nashville, Tennessee

22 *Commentary on the Whole Bible* (based upon Jameson, Faucet and Brown commentary, Zondervan Publishers, Grand Rapids Michigan, © 1997

23 Ernest K. Emurian, *Living Stories of Famous Hymns*, Baker Books, 1955, a division of Baker Book House Company, P.O. Box 6287, Grand Rapids, MI 49516-6287.

CHAPTER 7

24 Marie Curie, http://thinkexist.com/quotation/life_is_not_easy_for_any_of_us-but_what_of_that/9171.html

25 http://www.stanford.edu/group/king/frequentdocs/birmingham.pdf_

26 *www.lyrics007.com/**Jim**%20**Croce**%20Lyrics/**Time**%20In%20A%20**Bottle**%20Lyrics.html*

27 Chris Maxwell, "Ministries Today," Jul/Aug 2006, "Runaway Shepherds? Pastor dropouts make easy targets for criticism. But who's really to blame for ministry attrition?"

CHAPTER 8

28 Annie Lamont, as quoted on http://www.motivationalquotes.com/pages/hope-quotes.html

CHAPTER 9

29 Alvin Toffler, *Future Shock,* Random House, New York, New York, © 1970, Pg. 367

30 J. B. Lightfoot, *The Apostolic Fathers,* Baker House Publishers, Grand Rapids, MI, © 1956, Pg. 63

ABOUT THE AUTHOR

BILL WILSON IS THE Founder and Senior Pastor of "Metro Ministries," the world's largest Sunday School, and an international Christian humanitarian organization with headquarters in Brooklyn, NY. "Metro" reaches more than 40,000 inner-city children and their families every week in New York City and around the world. Based on his principle that "it is easier to build boys and girls than to repair men and women," this successful, relationship-centered pattern is currently recognized as one of the top ten influential ministries having the greatest impact around the world today.

Abandoned at 12 years old by his alcoholic mother, Bill's body still bears the scars of several childhood disorders. The painful beginning to his story is the same one he hears from the children he now reaches out to—that they have been abandoned by their families, society and even the agencies who are supposed to care for them. From a timid young boy, he has grown into a messenger of hope in the extreme darkness of today's inner city...and the price for his commitment has been high.

"Pastor Bill," as he is known to the kids, has been hospitalized repeatedly and continues to be treated for a gunshot wound to his mouth and jaw following a robbery. Personal adversity has only strengthened his resolve to do "whatever it takes." Bill Wilson has always believed that what happens *in* you is more important than what happens *to* you.

In 2007, renovations began on the "Metro World Ministries Center." Upon completion, this building will provide facilities to add programs that include obtaining a GED, parenting classes, and food services, as well as Bill Wilson's extensive training program that has proved successful in duplicating his commitment to reach millions of children with the love of Christ.

Pastor Bill speaks at leadership conferences and pastor's schools around the world focusing on reaching families, children, and the cities they live in. His book, **Whose Child Is This?** has been translated in 25 languages and his weekly television program, "In the Crosshairs," began airing in 2005. Check local listings for broadcast times in your area. The curriculum developed through this ministry is tested and proven in the hardcore, inner-city culture of New York before being translated into four languages and utilized in hundreds of cities worldwide using Bill Wilson's unique concept of "Sidewalk Sunday School."